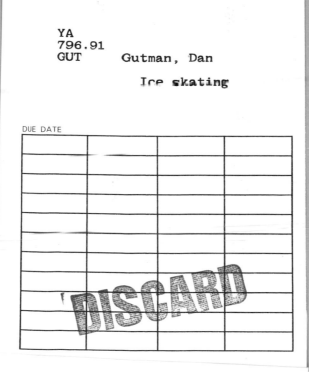

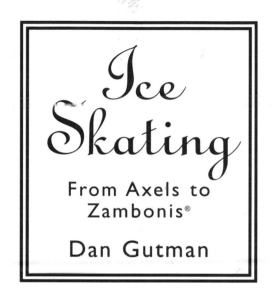

Ice Skating

From Axels to Zambonis®

Dan Gutman

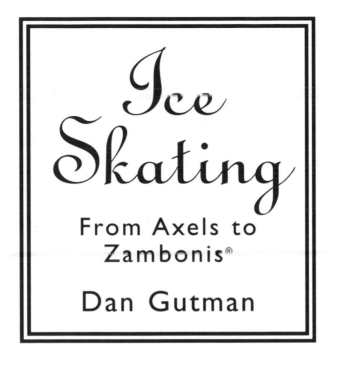

Ice Skating

From Axels to Zambonis®

Dan Gutman

Viking

VIKING
Published by the Penguin Group
Penguin Books USA Inc., 375 Hudson Street, New York, New York 10014, U.S.A.
Penguin Books Ltd, 27 Wrights Lane, London W8 5TZ, England
Penguin Books Australia Ltd, Ringwood, Victoria, Australia
Penguin Books Canada Ltd, 10 Alcorn Avenue, Toronto, Ontario, Canada M4V 3B2
Penguin Books (N.Z.) Ltd, 182-190 Wairau Road, Auckland 10, New Zealand

Penguin Books Ltd, Registered Offices: Harmondsworth, Middlesex, England

First published in the United States of America by Viking, a division of Penguin Books USA Inc., 1995

1 3 5 7 9 10 8 6 4 2

LIBRARY OF CONGRESS CATALOGING-IN-PUBLICATION DATA
Gutman, Dan.
Ice Skating : from axels to Zambonis / by Dan Gutman.   p.   cm.
Includes bibliographical references and index.
Summary : Introduces the history, famous performers, anecdotes,
and trivia of the sport of ice skating.
ISBN 0-670-86013-1
1. Skating — Juvenile literature. [1. Ice skating.]   I. Title.
GV849.G88 1995 796.91—dc20   95-14598 CIP AC

Printed in U.S.A.
Set in Weiss

Dedicated to John Tido and Richard Milner

Also by Dan Gutman

For Young Readers

Taking Flight (with Vicki Van Meter)

They Came from Centerfield

World Series Classics

Baseball's Greatest Games

Baseball's Biggest Bloopers: The Games That Got Away

For Adults

Banana Bats & Ding-Dong Balls:
A Century of Unique Baseball Inventions

Baseball Babylon: From the Black Sox to Pete Rose,
the Real Stories Behind the Scandals That Rocked the Game

It Ain't Cheatin' If You Don't Get Caught:
Scuffing, Spitting, Gunking, Razzing, and
Other Fundamentals of Our National Pastime

Super Memory: A Quick-Action Program for Memory Improvement
(with Dr. Douglas J. Herrmann)

I Didn't Know You Could Do That with a Computer!

Acknowledgments

This book could not have been written without the cooperation and assistance of Beth Davis at the World Figure Skating Museum and Hall of Fame in Colorado Springs, Colorado.

Others who played an important role in making this book possible were: Nat Andriani of The Associated Press; Carey Agans; Joan Curtis of the Cherry Hill Library; Liza Dey; Lisa Gonzales of Frank J. Zamboni & Company; Lynn Copley Graves and Jim Graves of Platoro Press; Paul and Michelle Harvath; Beat Hasler of the International Skating Union in Switzerland; Carol Heiss Jenkins; Jack, Pat, and Tara Lipinski; at Viking Children's Books, Elizabeth Law, Regina Hayes, Nina Putignano, Becky Laughlin, Margaret Mirabile, Janet Pascal, and Phil Airoldi; Kristin Matta; Doug Otto; Barry Rothman; Joan Vinson; Liza Voges and Julie Alperen at Kirchoff Wohlberg; Anna May Walker; and Nina Wallace, who dug through all that microfilm.

Thanks to all.

Contents

Introduction

The arena is completely dark as you glide out to the middle of the ice. The crowd is still buzzing about the last skater's performance, so you have a moment to think.

You flash back to the first time you pulled on a pair of ice skates. You were only 4 or 5 years old. When you took those first wobbly steps on the ice, you were frightened, grabbing onto your parents' hands to steady you on your feet.

But almost instantly you felt comfortable. The ice below you was as smooth as glass. You felt a sense of exhilaration. The wind split open to let you through. Swirling. Gliding. It was the closest thing to flying that you had ever experienced. Gravity was your partner, not your enemy.

Skating gave you a feeling of power and freedom. You fell in love with it immediately. That first day, you knew you wanted to be a skater.

You never realized how tough it would be—getting up at four in the morning to skate before school. Endless hours of practice in cold rinks when all the other kids were home huddled under warm covers. Back to the rink after school. Ballet lessons, gymnastics, weight training. Going to bed before all the good TV shows came on—so you could wake up in time to do it all over again the next day. You'll always feel a touch of resentment because you missed out on the childhood other kids enjoyed.

Skating was so easy to learn and so difficult to master. But you did it. You had to develop the grace of a matador and the personality of a bull. Now you're one of the best in the world. Everything you put into getting this far was worth it.

Here you are. A dozen years of training have led up to this moment. In the next 4 minutes and 30 seconds, more people are going to be watching you than any other person on the planet.

This is it. There are no second chances in skating. It's not like the World Series or the NBA Finals, where athletes can mess up three games and still win the seven-game series. One little trip, one little slip, and your chance for a medal is probably blown. Your career may be over.

A bead of sweat rolls down your forehead, and you haven't even taken your first step yet.

Suddenly a single white spotlight hits you. A booming voice announces your name. A hush of anticipation rises up from the audience. You take one deep breath and watch it rush out of your mouth. The music swells. And you push off. . . .

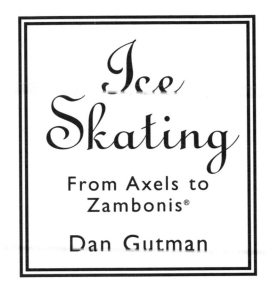

Ice Skating

From Axels to Zambonis®

Dan Gutman

1

⟨◇⟩

In the Beginning . . .

THE INVENTION OF SKATING

Who was the first caveman, cavewoman, or cavechild to strap on a pair of skates and glide across a patch of ice? We'll never know. We *do* know, however, that a pair of primitive skates was found at the bottom of a Swiss lake, and scientists calculated that they were made around 3000 B.C. It's the oldest pair of skates in the world.

The poor Swiss skater who tumbled through the ice that day probably wasn't out for a relaxing spin around the lake. The earliest skaters took up skating because they *had* to. They had to escape from enemies trying to kill them. They had to hunt for food. They had to get out of the cold as quickly as possible. With lakes and rivers frozen solid during the long winter months, skating was the fastest way to get around.

The ancient Romans and Greeks developed many things, but they didn't know anything about skating. They didn't have to know anything about it. It was the people up north who developed the sport and art of skating.

Historians believe the people of Finland were actually the *first* to skate. Other people referred to them as the "Skrid

Finnai" or "Sliding Finns." An ancient Finnish poem is the
first written reference to skating:

I fight with courage;
I keep a firm seat on horseback;
I am skilled in swimming;
I glide along the ice on skates;
I excel in darting the lance;
I am dextrous with the oar;
and yet a Russian maid disdains me!

BONY SKATES

The first skates were made, not from steel, but from the
long leg bones of large animals—horses, deer, elk, and sheep.
In fact, the English word "skate" is derived from the German
word "schake," which means "shank" or "leg bone." Even
today, skates in Holland are called "schenkel" or "leg bone."

Ancient skate-makers bored a hole in each end of the
bones and slipped leather straps through the holes to attach
the bones to shoes. The skater would grease the bottoms
with hog lard to make them more slippery.

It was impossible to "push off" the ice with skates made from
bones. So early skaters used pointed sticks to shove themselves
forward, the same way cross-country skiiers do. Skiing on snow
and skating on ice were developed around the same time.

Skates made from bone have been found in Germany,
Sweden, England, and other parts of Europe. In North America, the Iroquois Indians chased deer across frozen Canadian
lakes on skates of bone.

THE IRON AGE

It was the people of Holland who made skating a way of life. Centuries ago, as now, the towns of Holland were connected by canals. These canals were frozen for months at a time during the winter, effectively shutting down the Dutch economy. Making the best of a bad situation, the resourceful Dutch took up skating and used the canals like speed-skating tracks to get around.

It was the Dutch who were the first to replace bone skates with skates made from iron. Sharp iron blades could grip the ice, so skaters no longer had to push themselves forward with poles. Instead they learned to push off their left skate and glide on the right, and then push off the right skate and glide on the left. This technique, which is the way we skate to this day, came to be called "the Dutch Roll."

THE EARLIEST KNOWN SKATING IMAGE

We know the ancient Dutch knew the Dutch Roll because the man in the background is clearly doing it in this picture, the earliest known skating image. It depicted an event that took place in 1396; it was made in 1498 by the Dutch artist Johannes Brugman.

The picture is of Lydwine, a beautiful 16-year-old girl who lived in the Dutch town of Schiedam. Legend has it that some friends came to visit Lydwine before the feast of Candlemas and invited her to go skating. She wasn't feeling up to it, but her friends insisted. Once they were on the ice, one of her friends promptly knocked Lydwine down, breaking six

Lydwine takes a spill.

of her ribs. Medicine being what it was in those days, poor Lydwine was bedridden for the rest of her life.

After the accident, Lydwine had visions and was credited with performing many miracles, including some that occurred after she passed away in 1433. Lydwine was canonized in 1890. In 1944 she was named the patron saint of skating.

A WAR ON ICE

The Dutch were so good on ice that they prevailed in the only military battle fought on skates, the Battle of IJsselmeer in 1572. Holland was in a bloody conflict with Spain, and they were getting the worst of it. The Dutch fleet was frozen in at Amsterdam harbor, and it looked like they were finished. Spanish commander Don Frederick sent his troops out to storm the Dutch vessels and take Amsterdam by sea.

The Dutch musketeers, however, had grown up whizzing over the ice-covered canals of Holland. Quickly, they strapped on their wooden skates with iron blades and glided out of their ships to wage one last, desperate battle. The Spaniards, taken by surprise and totally outmaneuvered by the swift Dutch skaters, were wiped out. Hundreds of their dead were left on the ice.

Don Frederick was so impressed that he ordered 7,000 pairs of skates for the soldiers he had left. A year later, however, he abandoned the idea. His Spanish troops just couldn't get the knack of skating in formation.

A VERY PRETTY ART

The Dutch brought skating to nearby England, and in the year 1180 this passage appeared in William FitzStephen's *Description of the Most Noble City of London*:

> When the great fenne or moore (which watereth the walls of the citie on the North side) is frozen, many young men play on the yce, some striding as wide as they may, doe glide swiftlie; some tye bones to their feete and under their heeles, and shoving themselves with a little picked staff do slide as swiftlie as a birde flyeth in the aire or an arrow out of a cross-bow.

Skating didn't catch on in England right away. The English didn't *need* to skate, as the Dutch did. For the next 500 years, there was no mention of skating in English literature.

Then, in 1662, British Lord of the Admiralty Samuel Pepys spent an afternoon in St. James Park and afterward penned this note in his diary:

> Dec. 1. To my Lord Sandwich's, to Mr. Moore and then over the Parke, where I first in my life, it being a great frost, did see people sliding with their skeates, which is a very pretty art.

Londoners had discovered that skating was not only a good way to move from place to place in the wintertime; it was also *fun*. When the British established their colonies in America, they brought their skates with them.

"I have seen some Officers of the British Army, at Boston, and some of the Army at Cambridge, skait with perfect Elegance," John Adams wrote to his son in 1780.

Skating continued to spread around the world, or at least to the colder parts of the world. Marie Antoinette is said to have skated in 1776. Napoleon supposedly strapped on a pair of skates in 1781. In the 1850s and 1860s, skating became a full-fledged craze in Europe and America. In the rink at New York's Central Park, 50,000 people a *day* would go skating. Men and women of all classes joined one another on the ice.

Philadelphia was the center of skating in the United States, and by 1867, there were nine skating clubs there. The first one was founded on December 21, 1849.

Club members were required to skate with a 60-foot cord and reel in case they had to fish a fallen skater out of Philadelphia's Schuylkill River. Rescuers were paid $12 per

The skating craze gripped Europe and America during the 1850s and 60s.

life they saved (and they were fined $1 if caught without their equipment). By 1869, the Philadelphia Skating Club and Humane Society boasted it had saved 259 skaters from drowning.

EARLY SKATES

Ice skates went from bone to wood to iron to steel. But the biggest problem was fastening the skate securely to the skater's foot. For centuries, leather straps were used, but these quickly became loose and skaters would frequently sprain their ankles. By the 1800s, straps were being built into the skate itself, like a sandal.

What skaters really needed was a skate that firmly at-

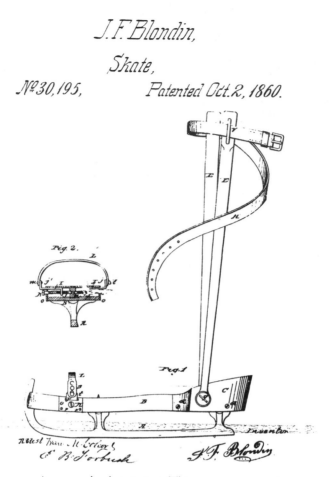

U.S. Patent Office

*A very early skate patent. This one was supposed
to provide strong ankle support.*

tached to the skater's boot. That came along in 1850, when a
Philadelphian named E. V. Bushnell invented a strapless
skate—the blades clipped right to the boot. His invention
revolutionized skating because for the first time skaters could
twist, turn, spin, and leap without losing their blades.

American inventors turned their attention to skating, and
149 patents were issued during the 1860s for new skate de-

No. 9R4985 Ladies' Skate. The runners are made from **welded iron and steel hardened.** Plate clamp and levers of best quality **cold rolled steel.** All parts polished and **nickel plated.** Sizes, 8¼ to 10¼ inches. Price, per pair.......**$2.38**
When ordering skates give length of shoe in inches.

Collection of the author

Skates advertised in the 1902 Sears, Roebuck & Company catalog.

signs. Over those years, the front of the blade went from a graceful curve to a sharp point, which enabled skaters to perform more elaborate acrobatics. "Toe picks," those sharp teeth you see in the front of blades, would not appear until the 1880s.

Skates were usually sold in hardware stores. During the skating craze of the 1860s, one could buy a pair of ice skates for as little as 75 cents. A top-of-the-line pair sold for about $6. Back then, it cost 15 cents to skate in a public rink for a day, or $2 a year ($1 for kids). Of course, many people simply skated on frozen lakes and ponds for free.

In the 1902 Sears, Roebuck & Co. catalog, 14 different styles of skates were offered, ranging from 43 cents ("The toe and heel plates and all clamps are made of the **best quality of cold roll homogeneous steel**") to $3.25 speed skates ("**This skate is made under the personal supervision of Mr. Joseph F. Donoghue, world's champion skater** . . . and has been used for the past five years in **winning all his great races** and making his **wonderful records,** and his success is as much due to the perfection of these skates as to his own skill.").

Around the turn of the century, skates with the boot and blade attached as one unit appeared for the first time.

Over the last 100 years, aside from a few minor improvements, skates have remained pretty much the same.

ROLLER SKATING

People found skating to be so much fun that they wanted to do it even in warm weather. Inventors began working on a new kind of skate that would glide on land the same way steel blades glide on ice.

In 1760, a Belgian musical instrument maker named Joseph Merlin rigged up the first, primitive pair of skates with wheels on them.

Merlin had been invited to a masquerade ball, and he thought that would be the perfect occasion to introduce his new invention. Mounted on the skates, Merlin sailed into the ballroom while playing a violin. The guests were charmed.

Unfortunately, Merlin had not yet figured out how to turn or stop on his roller skates, and he went crashing into a floor-to-ceiling mirror. The mirror, violin, skates, and Merlin himself were shattered, though he survived.

Other inventors tried to build working roller skates, but they weren't perfected until 1863, when James L. Plimpton of New York designed a pair. The first roller skates with ball bearings came out in 1875, and a new form of skating captured the public's imagination.

About a hundred years after roller skates were born, surfers looking for a way to surf year-round developed another new sport—skateboarding.

In-line skates, or Rollerblades, which are so popular today, were actually first invented in 1823 by an English fruit salesman named Robert John Tyers.

DID YOU KNOW . . .

• One of the earliest speed-skating races took place in Prickwillow, England, on January 4, 1821. An English sportsman named Woodward challenged the fastest skater in the world, J. Gittam of Holland, to skate a straight mile in less than 3 minutes. Gittam took off from a flying start and crossed the finish line with 7 seconds to spare.

• Dutch children used to play a game on skates in which they would whack a small ball around an obstacle course with a long club. They called the game "Kolven" and the club a "kolf."

This, according to one legend anyway, was how the game of golf began.

• A skate is "scatch" in Old English, "sschaat" in Flemish, "Schlittschuh" in German, "skoite" in Danish, and "le patin" in French.

• There was plenty of ice to go around, so to speak, in skating's formative years. It was so cold in A.D. 975 that half the population of France froze to death. From 1400 to 1800 Europe endured what has been called a "little ice age." Even the canals of Venice were frozen for a time. In the Great Frost of 1683 the Thames River in London was frozen solid for three months.

2

⚬⚭⚬

Skating Becomes a Sport

The Dutch made skating a part of their daily life, but it was the British who turned it into a sport and an art form.

Dutch skates were designed for long-distance skating through the canals of Holland. The blades were long and flat, like today's speed skates. But England didn't have canals to skate on. It had ponds. To skate on small bodies of water, English skaters required shorter, curved blades to make tight turns.

Around 1770 the British developed "fluted skates"—blades with a groove down the middle to give each foot an inside and outside edge, like the skates used today.

For a long time, the novelty of gliding on skates over ice was enough to make skating a popular recreation activity. But going around and around in circles on a pond does get to be monotonous, and British skaters who had mastered the hobby began looking for something more challenging. They began skating in specific patterns, or "figures." That's why the sport is called "figure skating." These figures, carved in the ice by the sharp blades, would remain on the ice when the skater completed them.

World Figure Skating Museum and Hall of Fame

The design shown here is the official logo of the World Figure Skating Hall of Fame and Museum in Colorado Springs, Colorado. It's not simply an attractive pattern. It's the figure carved in the ice by British skater Charles Arthur Cumming during the 1908 Olympic Games. Cumming won the silver medal that year—the first time the Olympic Games included figure skating.

The British have always had a reputation for being somewhat formal, and by the 1850s the "English Style" had come to dominate skating. Skaters were stiff and precise as they carved their perfect figures. Competitions were held for the first time, and the winners were those who could trace and retrace the most complicated, symmetrical, and exact figures in the ice. Skaters didn't jump, spin, or throw their arms and legs about dramatically. They drew *pictures* on the ice.

Skating didn't look like dance. In fact, it looked almost like drudgery.

JACKSON HAINES

Then along came the mysterious Jackson Haines, the first in a long line of great figure skaters.

Haines was born in 1840 in Chicago, or perhaps in New York. It all depends on whom you believe. As a boy he studied music and dance. When he took up skating, he didn't like the rigid English Style. He made one simple discovery that would change the sport forever—*skating could be combined with dancing.*

Haines skated with style, flinging his arms and legs about, leaping off the ice, and spinning in circles. It must have been shocking in its time. He was the first person to skate with musical accompaniment, and he even had music written specially for his routines. He used ornate sets. He wore fancy costumes while he skated, dressing sometimes as a woman, or even a bear.

Haines was flamboyant, and he knew how to work a crowd. Before he stepped on the ice, he would dramatically dip his blades into boiling water. He would skate out from under his cap, and then pick it up off the ice without interrupting his routine. At the end of the performance, he would lean over backwards until his head touched the ice, then doff his cap to the crowd.

Naturally, Haines was blasted by critics for paying more attention to his form than to his figures. "Toesteps, spins, and pirouettes can hardly be described as skating, in the English sense of the word," sniffed British skating authority G. Herbert Fowler.

Feeling unappreciated in America, Haines decided to take

World Figure Skating Museum and Hall of Fame

Jackson Haines.

his art overseas. Leaving his wife Alma and three children behind, he set off for Europe. He was just 24 years old, and he would never return to the United States.

Haines put on exhibitions in London, Paris, Stockholm, and Moscow. He was an expert roller skater, and performed an opera, *Le Prophète*, on roller skates. By the time he got to Vienna, Austria, in 1866, he was an international celebrity. Ice rinks were built for him. Babies were named after him.

Haines settled in Vienna and his new style of skating came to be called "the Viennese School."

Like so many other rebels, Jackson Haines died young. Some accounts of his life say he contracted pneumonia. Others say he died with his skating boots on, after breaking a leg jumping over a chair.

In any case, he passed away in Finland sometime around 1875. He is buried in the little Finnish village of Gamla-Karleby. His tombstone reads simply, "Jackson Haines—The American Skate King."

Besides the fact that he revolutionized skating style, Jackson Haines was the first to attach blades *permanently* to his skating boots. His all-in-one skates were ridiculed at the time, but they clearly gave the skater better control and stability. In time all skates would be made that way. He is also credited with inventing the sit spin.

Seven years after Jackson Haines passed away, the first international skating competition was held in Vienna. The grand prize was a statue of Haines. It was won by Leopold Frey, who had learned how to skate from Jackson Haines.

AXEL PAULSEN

The day Leopold Frey won the first international skating competition, a young Norwegian man startled the crowd with a dramatic flying jump. Skating swiftly, he pushed off the outside edge of his left skate to get airborne. He turned one full revolution in the air, and then another half revolution. Finally he landed on his right skate, skating backwards. Nobody had ever seen such an athletic leap on ice before.

The skater only placed third in the competition, but his

Axel Paulsen .

name—Axel Paulsen—is remembered both inside and outside the figure skating community even today. You've probably heard of that revolutionary jump he invented—the *axel*.
Today the axel is called "the king of jumps." (See Chapter 5
for more about the axel and other jumps.)

Axel Paulson was not only a great figure skater; he was
also the top speed skater of his day. He won the first international speed-skating competition in 1885 and held many
of the records for distances ranging from 1,500 to 15,000
meters throughout the 1880s.

Paulsen also designed a speed skate with a thin blade and
a tubular support design that was longer and lighter than
other speed skates of its day. Modern speed and hockey
skates are made the same basic way.

THE FIRST OLYMPIC GAMES

When the International Olympic Committee gathered in 1895 to pick the events of the first modern Olympics, they chose figure skating. Unfortunately, there wasn't enough ice to skate on at the Olympics in Athens (1896), Paris (1900), or St. Louis (1904). Finally, in 1908, figure skating became the first winter sport to be a part of the Olympic Games, in London.

Figure skating was not included in the 1912 or 1916 Olympics because of a conflict with another winter tournament, the Nordic Games. In 1920 in Antwerp, Belgium, skating became a part of the Olympics for good. Four years later, the Olympics were divided into summer games and winter games.

A complete listing of "The Champions: Olympic, World, and United States" follows Chapter 7.

ULRICH SALCHOW

Skating's next great innovator was Sweden's Ulrich Salchow, who, like Axel Paulsen, devised a jump that bears his name. (Chapter 5 includes a description of the salchow.) Salchow won ten World Championships (from 1901 to 1911) and nine European Championships. When figure skating became an Olympic event for the first time in 1908, Salchow won the gold medal easily.

Salchow wasn't beaten until he was 42, by a 26-year-old Swedish architect named Gillis Grafstrom. It was Grafstrom who developed the flying sit spin, forward inside spiral, and other innovative jumps and spins. He would go on to win three straight Olympic gold medals (1920, 1924, and 1928) and one silver (1932).

WOMEN TAKE TO THE ICE

The practice of skating is peculiarly adapted to give our females that outdoor recreation they so much need. It expands the chest, strengthens the hips, and invigorates the entire system. If young ladies would become good skaters, they would be much better fitted to become mothers of American children.
— The Skater's Manual, *1867*

MADGE SYERS

In 1902, a young Englishwoman named Madge Syers had the audacity to enter the World Figure Skating Championship in London. There wasn't any rule barring women from competitive skating. The tournament was open to *all* skaters. It was just that nobody ever thought a woman would enter. The *idea* of a woman participating in such a strenuous athletic event was unheard of. Women simply were not considered athletic.

As it turned out, Madge Syers finished second to the great Ulrich Salchow, and many observers felt she deserved first place.

To prevent future embarrassments like that, in 1906, figure skating officials instituted a separate championship for women. Naturally, Madge Syers won it. She won again in 1907, and in 1908 she won the gold medal in the Olympics.

World Figure Skating Museum and Hall of Fame

Madge Syers, the first great female skater.

Skating has long been promoted as a good exercise. But it took quite a while for many men (and women, for that matter) to become comfortable with women skating. In the 1700s, an American schoolteacher was charged with witchcraft for teaching young women to skate. In Germany, a woman was stoned to death for skating in 1851.

When the French ambassador to the Netherlands, Comte D'avaux, saw a Dutch princess skating in a "daring" outfit, he reported to Louis XIV, "Twas a very extraordinary thing to see the Princess of Orange clad in petticoats shorter than are generally worn by ladies so strictly decorous, these tucked up half-way to her waist, and with iron pattens on her feet learning to slide sometime poised on one leg sometime on another."

Still, skating buffs soon realized that women were just as good as—if not better than—men on ice. Visitors to the Netherlands were warned, "When skating in Holland, be careful how you show off your speed before a lady, or you may have the pleasure of following in her wake instead of being her leader."

Only in recent decades has it been completely acceptable for women to compete at sports. Today, of course, skating is one of the few sports (along with gymnastics) in which women receive more attention, acclaim, television ratings, and money than men.

But hardly anyone remembers the woman who started it all, Madge Syers.

CHARLOTTE

The first skater to become a worldwide celebrity was a German woman named Charlotte Oelschlagel. She was so famous in her time that she was known throughout the world by her first name alone.

Charlotte never skated competitively, preferring to put on exhibitions to entertain audiences. She had golden hair down to her ankles, and like Jackson Haines before her, she knew how to put on a show.

In 1915, Charlotte, just 17 years old, was scheduled to perform for six weeks at New York's Hippodrome, then the largest theater in America. Her show, which also included 40 other skaters, was so popular that it packed in 6,000 people twice a day for three years. It was the first ice show, and it set the stage for the Ice Capades, Holiday on Ice, the Ice Follies, and others.

Besides skating individually, she performed a dramatic ballet with Curt Neumann in which she became a dying swan on ice. The couple originated the "death spiral" spin—the one in which the lady is held by her legs and spun in a wide circle so her head nearly scrapes the ice. Later, Charlotte and Neumann would become husband and wife.

Charlotte also appeared in the first skating movie, a silent thriller called *The Frozen Warning*. The plot hinged on Charlotte's spelling out the word S-P-I-E-S in the ice.

YOU CAN'T HAVE ICE SKATING WITHOUT ICE

For centuries after skating began, the sport could only be enjoyed outdoors in very cold weather, and only where there was a body of water covered by a thick layer of ice. Ice skating would never have become a worldwide sport if somebody had not developed a way to create ice artificially indoors.

We take it for granted now, but producing ice without natural freezing temperatures was a huge accomplishment in the ninetenth century.

It was well known that evaporation could produce intense cold, so many inventors used that as a starting point in their effort to create artificial ice. In 1842 an Englishman named Henry Kirk mixed crystallized alum, salts, and melted sulphur in a London cellar to make a small ice floor he called his "miniature alpine lake."

To make it more slippery, he coated the floor with hog's grease. The place smelled awful, and Kirk's ice was cut up very quickly by skates. But it attracted much attention, and other scientists started thinking of a way to make frozen water.

In 1865 W. A. Parker used brine and carbonic acid to produce ice thick enough to withstand a skate. Soon after, a New Yorker named Matthew Julius Bujac buried metal tubes in a bed of concrete below the surface of water and circulated ammonia gas, ether, and carbonic acid through the tubes. The system was primitive, but it worked.

Professor John Gamgee of England improved on the refrigeration process, and installed a 24×16-foot rink in a room in Chelsea, England.

The first full-sized rink using Gamgee's process—the Glaciarium—opened in 1876 in Manchester. It was bumpy and damp, and a thick mist wafted around the rink, but you could skate on it. When Thomas Edison invented his phonograph the next year and the incandescent light bulb three years later, indoor skating at night with musical accompaniment became possible.

Gamgee's system was perfected in the 1890s, and ice rinks popped up in Frankfurt, Munich, Paris, London, and even Jersey City. Fancy hotels installed ice rinks on their roofs. By 1904, rinks had appeared in Australia, South Africa, and other warm parts of the world where people had hardly ever *seen* ice. Finally, figure skating was a sport that *anybody* could enjoy, night or day, regardless of the weather.

Today, skating outside on a frozen pond is a special thrill

that makes you feel like you're living in a different century. Most of today's skaters rarely set foot on natural ice.

EVERYTHING YOU ALWAYS WANTED TO KNOW ABOUT THE ZAMBONI®

- What's a Zamboni? The enormous, lumbering machine that resurfaces ice rinks.
- Why is it called Zamboni? It was invented by Frank Zamboni of Paramount, California, in 1947. He wanted to name his company Paramount Engineering Company, but that name was already taken. So he named his company and his machine after himself.
- How did he invent the Zamboni? Zamboni ran an ice factory in the 1920s. When home refrigerators

The Zamboni is so popular that it was made into a trading card.

became available and people no longer needed to buy ice, he opened up an ice rink. Seeing that it took six workers with shovels an hour and a half to resurface the ice manually, Zamboni decided to find a better way.

• How does a Zamboni work? First, a long blade shaves 1/16 of an inch off the surface of the ice. The shavings are collected in a large tank, and a device washes the surface and flushes dirt out of the grooves. Finally, a cloth spreads a thin film of hot water over the ice to leave it smooth as glass. It takes about 15 to 30 minutes to resurface a rink.

• How did the Zamboni become famous? Olympic star Sonja Henie saw the first Zamboni and asked Zamboni to make one for her traveling ice show. When rink managers around the country saw it, they began ordering them. In 1960 the whole world saw Zambonis on TV at the Winter Olympics, and the machine's fame spread further.

• How much does a Zamboni weigh? 6,480 pounds.

• How many Zambonis are there? The company makes seven models, including the Astro-Zamboni, which sucks water up from artificial turf fields. Altogether they have manufactured more than 5,000 Zambonis and sold them to 33 countries around the world, including 11 to China, 200 to Japan, and 900 throughout Europe.

• How many Zambonis are made each year? About 200. Each Zamboni is handmade, and they must be ordered six months in advance.

- How long does a Zamboni last? Ten to twenty years. A few have made it well into their thirties before breaking down.
- How much does a Zamboni cost? $50,000 for the top-of-the-line model.
- How fast does a Zamboni go? Eight miles an hour. Zambonis are powered by Volkswagen 1.8 litre, 4-cylinder engines.
- What's the worst thing that ever happened to a Zamboni? Hockey player Ulf Samuelsson, a defenseman for Hartford, once became frustrated and attacked a Zamboni with an ice squeegee. He didn't do much damage, though.
- Are Zambonis hazardous to your health? In 1989, researchers in Quebec described "Zamboni Syndrome," an ailment in which 135 players, cheerleaders, and spectators got nitrogen-dioxide poisoning at a hockey game. The cure was a tune-up for the Zamboni and better ventilation for the ice rink.
- What's the strangest place to find a Zamboni? In *Peanuts*, a Zamboni resurfaced the ice on Woodstock's bird bath.
- There must be Zamboni T-shirts, right? Yes, and Zamboni baseball caps, pins, belt buckles, key rings, coffee mugs, and bumper stickers (MY OTHER CAR IS A ZAMBONI). Write Zamboni at P.O. Box 770, Paramount, CA 90723 for a catalog.
- Is Frank Zamboni still alive? No, he passed away in 1988. In his 87 years, Frank Zamboni never learned how to skate.

DID YOU KNOW . . .

• The first skating club was formed in Edinburgh, Scotland, around 1700. To become a member of the club, one had to skate a complete circle on either foot, and then jump over three hats. Women were not allowed in the club, and the men wore white ties, tails, and tall hats while skating.

• The game of hockey goes back even further than skating. The Greeks played a form of the game, on dry land, in 500 B.C. In the 1700s, hockey was played in France and taken to Canada by French refugees. It was adopted as an official game at McGill University there in 1879.

Nobody knows for sure why the game is called "hockey," but there are a few theories. "Hawkey" was a feast at harvest time in England during the 1500s. "Hoquet" is French for a shepherd's staff, a bent stick that looks a little bit like a hockey stick.

The most interesting theory claims that in 1740 French explorers sailing up the St. Laurence River saw Iroquois Indians playing a game in which they hit a hard ball with a stick. Every so often players would shout "Ho-gee!" which was translated as "It hurts!"

That's the legend, anyway.

• The Olympic symbol looks like it could be a skating figure, but it's not. The five rings linked together represent the sporting friendship of all peoples on the five continents (Europe, Asia, Africa, Australia, and America). Each ring is a different color—red, green, black, yellow, and blue.

• At the 1920 Olympics in Antwerp, Belgium, the entire United States figure skating team consisted of two people, Theresa Weld and Nathaniel Niles. They competed in singles and as a pair. Weld became the first American skater to win an Olympic medal, the bronze. Niles finished sixth. As a pair, Weld and Niles finished fourth.

3

∞

The First Superstars

SONJA HENIE

Before there was a Nancy Kerrigan or Elvis Stojko, there was a Sonja Henie. Before there was a Katarina Witt, or Dorothy Hamill, Peggy Fleming, or all the rest, there was a Sonja Henie.

She was the first worldwide celebrity skater. The first skater whose fame went far beyond the ice. She made Charlotte look like a weekend skater. Sonja Henie was the first female sports legend.

It was the middle of a blizzard in 1912 when Sonja was born in Oslo, the capital of Norway. Soon after she learned to walk, she wanted to skate. She begged and pleaded, but her parents insisted she was too young. Sonja's older brother, Leif, was a skater, and she was jealous.

Finally, when she turned six, Sonja's parents said they would get her a pair of ice skates, the kind with double runners. Sonja refused them. She didn't want "baby" skates. She wanted *real* skates.

And that's what she got.

At Frogner Stadium in Oslo, Leif taught her the basics. "If you're going to skate," he said, "you're going to fall." Leif taught her how to relax her body and fall down like a length of rope instead of like a stick of wood.

Sonja didn't fall very often. She had a good feeling for balance and rhythm, and soon she was better than Leif. She loved skating so much that she would go to Frogner early in the morning and sometimes forget to come home for dinner.

While she was learning to skate, Sonja was also discovering a love of ballet. She put on shows in her living room, complete with tickets and music. After she ushered in her parents, she would turn on the record player and dance for their applause.

Ballet lessons followed, and Sonja began to incorporate dancing into her ice skating.

She was just 7 when the top skaters at Frogner began to notice her talent. They taught her how to trace figures in the ice, and she became so good at it that she could etch the same figure ten times, leaving just one line on the patch of ice.

That same year, Sonja entered her first competition, skating against children nearly twice her age. She won, and took home a silver paper cutter as her prize.

It was obvious to everyone who saw her skate that Sonja was a child prodigy. By the time she was 10 years old, she was the champion of Norway. And Norway is a nation of ice skaters.

The 1924 Olympics were held in Chamonix, France. Though she was only 11, Sonja decided to enter.

All the other skaters wore plain, black, ankle-length skirts and skated slow, dull routines. Sonja hit the ice in a short, white satin dress with shoulders trimmed in fur.

Shockingly, she included a move in which her feet (gasp!) left the ice. The judges were not amused. Jumps were not considered ladylike in 1924.

Sonja finished in last place. But everybody noticed the little girl with the fancy costume and exciting leaps.

She kept at it, and in 1927 Sonja Henie took first place in the World Figure Skating Championships at her hometown of Oslo. She was just 14 years old.

At the 1928 Olympics in St. Moritz, Switzerland, Sonja shocked the judges again when she introduced dance chore-ography into her free program. But the judges were more ap-preciative this time, and when the scores were tallied, 15-year-old Sonja Henie was the Olympic gold medalist in figure skating. After she heard she had won, she broke down and wept in the locker room.

In those days, skaters didn't turn professional after the Olympic Games. There was no such *thing* as a professional skater. There were no ice shows she could join. No million-dollar endorsement contracts. No television specials.

There was only one thing for a skater to do after winning the Olympic gold. Win it *again*. That's what Sonja Henie did in 1932 at Lake Placid. And to show the world that she was the greatest skater of her time, Sonja won the gold *again* in 1936 at Garmisch, Germany.

No woman had ever won three Olympic gold medals for figure skating, and nobody has since. In that period of time, Sonja also reeled off ten consecutive World Championships. She had totally dominated her sport for more than a decade, and she was still only 24 years old.

But the career of Sonja Henie was just getting started.

Sonja's ambition was to win more than medals and trophies. She wanted to bring figure skating to the *world*. She realized that people weren't interested in watching skaters trace figures in the ice. The public wanted *dancing* on ice. And she would give it to them.

A month after the 1936 Olympics, Sonja announced that she had decided to become a professional skater and would be touring the world with a traveling ice show.

The show was a sensation. Sixty skaters. Colorful costumes. Special-effects lighting. There was a whole lot of

Sonja Henie.

Sonja Henie, of course. Her trademark was a skating version of Pavlova's dying swan ballet.

People had never seen anything like it. In Chicago, more than a quarter of a million tickets were sold. Hundreds of customers had to be turned away. In Sweden the crowds were so anxious to see Sonja that the glass windows of her car were shattered by bodies pressing against it.

Having conquered the sport of figure skating and the stage, Sonja set her sights on another goal—Hollywood.

She rented a little rink in Los Angeles called the Polar Palace and sent a personal invitation to every bigwig in the movie business. The rink was jammed with studio heads and stars such as Mary Pickford, Douglas Fairbanks, John Barrymore, Spencer Tracy, Clark Gable, Ginger Rogers, Gary Cooper, and Bette Davis. It was like a Hollywood premiere.

Afterward, the movie offers poured in. Sonja held out for a starring role and was signed to a five year contract to make one movie a year for 20th Century-Fox.

In her first film, *One in a Million*, Sonja played a skater (surprise!) who is brought to the United States and rockets to stardom after a dazzling performance at Madison Square Garden. The skating scenes were shot on black ice so that Sonja wouldn't fade into the background.

One in a Million was a hit, and Sonja was suddenly one of Hollywood's hottest actresses. She would make ten more movies from 1937 to 1945, co-starring with actors such as Don Ameche, Cesar Romero, Tyrone Power, Ethel Merman, Ray Milland, and Rudy Vallee.

They were fluffy, silly movies, but people came to see

them. The movies made Sonja Henie a household name, and transformed skating from a sport to popular entertainment.

Altogether, the films made $25 million, and in 1939 Sonja Henie was making more money than any other woman in the world. She would earn $47 million in her career, much of which took place during the Depression.

As one of the first female superstars, Sonja was hounded by the press. She both loved and hated the attention. She was a flamboyant personality who would occasionally arrive at parties on an elephant. There were rumors that she drank a bit more than she should have. The newspapers gossiped about romances with Tyrone Power, Clark Gable, Joe Louis, and just about any other man she was seen with.

A photo of Sonja shaking hands with Adolph Hitler at the 1936 Olympics made her an outcast in her native Norway. The nation was conquered by the Germans in World War II, and many believed Sonja was a Nazi, or at the very least a Nazi sympathizer.

She moved to the United States and became an American citizen. In 1940 she married Dan Topping, the owner of the New York Yankees. Two other husbands followed, but no children. Sonja Henie died of leukemia in 1969.

Years earlier, a young Russian girl named Ludmila Pro-topopov saw a Sonja Henie movie titled *Sun Valley Serenade* and decided then and there that she wanted to become a skater. Ludmila went on to win two Olympic gold medals for pairs skating with her husband, Oleg.

That was Sonja Henie's biggest contribution to figure skating—she inspired thousands of girls and boys to take up the sport. Chances are, many of the people on the following pages strapped on their first pair of skates after seeing Sonja Henie glide so gracefully across the ice.

"She was able to inspire and enchant, and that is what it is all about," said skater John Curry. "Most people today could not begin to capture any of her kind of feeling or spirit."

"All my life I have wanted to skate, and all my life I have skated."

—Sonja Henie

DICK BUTTON

You probably think of Dick Button as the bald guy who shows up on TV to analyze figure skating competitions. In fact, a lot of the spectacular skating we see today is because of innovations Dick Button made nearly 50 years ago.

As a boy, Dick was uncoordinated and overweight. He got his first pair of hand-me-down skates from his older brothers George and Jack. They taught him how to skate on Coffin's Pond near their home in Englewood, New Jersey.

Dick loved skating so much that long after the ice was gone in the spring, he would still bring his skates to school, hoping by some miracle that he'd be able to go skating. Other boys made fun of him. Figure skating, many believed, was just something Sonja Henie did in a ballet costume.

Dick didn't take a formal lesson until he was 12 years old,

and it was a disaster. "You'll never learn to skate," his teacher told him. But the baby fat turned into muscle and Button developed into an athlete. Just six years after that first lesson, Dick Button had an Olympic gold medal hanging from his neck.

For Americans, it had been a long time coming. Shortly after Sonja Henie won her last gold medal in 1936, the world was engulfed in World War II. The Olympics was canceled in 1940 and 1944. Europeans, with their balletic style, ruled figure skating in those years.

But in the 12 years between Olympics, Button and other American men developed a new style. The emphasis was on athletics more than on dance. The Americans weren't content to do single turn jumps. They did doubles (two rotations in the air). Axels got longer and higher. Spins became faster and were done in combination with jumps.

The skating reflected the American personality—daring, inventive, energetic, extroverted, and aggressive. It was called "the American Style."

Dick Button and his coach, Gustave Lussi, led the way. Lussi had come to America from Switzerland when he was 20. He was a ski jumper who had turned to skating after a serious accident.

Each year, Button tried to perfect a new jump. In 1945, he figured out how to do a double salchow. In 1946, it was the double loop. In 1947, he introduced the double flip and double lutz. In 1948, he took on the double axel.

That was the most challenging—two and a half complete turns in the air. It had never been performed in international competition when Dick became determined to introduce it at the 1948 Olympics.

Try as hard as he could, Dick couldn't nail the double axel. He became so obsessed with the jump that he would do it in his sleep. Sometimes he would fall, and his family became used to hearing Dick leap from his bed in the middle of the night and crash to the floor.

After weeks and months of landing on his hips, Dick's body was black and blue. His parents begged him to give up the double axel. They were afraid he was going to hurt himself permanently.

But suddenly, the day before the Olympics, Button found the knack. He landed a perfect double axel in practice. He couldn't believe it, so he tried it again. Same result. He did it a dozen times, and each time the jump went smoothly.

The double axel was conquered. Now all he had to do was land it under the pressure of competition.

At 6,000 feet, the air was thin in St. Moritz, Switzerland. Dick became winded easily and would sometimes inhale oxygen before skating. He didn't do much warming up. He wanted to save his energy for when it counted.

The strains of *Roumanian Fantasy* began and Button began his routine. After two minutes, he was gasping for breath and felt like he was going to collapse. But after putting five years of work in, he wasn't going to stop because he was out of breath.

Up until a few seconds before it was scheduled in his program, Dick still wasn't sure he would attempt the double axel. At the moment of truth, he decided to go for it.

Dick Button in a flying sit spin.

The lift was strong, the revolutions complete, and the landing smooth. Perfect! It was as if Button was the first in the world to develop the atomic bomb. Now the rest of the skaters would have to catch up.

He was so tired he could barely push himself off the ice. The marks were high, with one judge awarding a perfect score of 6.0. There was no room for another skater to top Button's marks. He became the first American to win an Olympic gold medal in figure skating.

Dick Button was 18 at the time, and he was accepted by Harvard University. But he wasn't finished with his skating innovations just yet. In 1949 he introduced the double loop/double loop. In 1950, it was the triple double loop (a "triple double" is a double jump repeated three times without steps in between). In 1951 he pulled off a double axel/double loop combination.

Shortly after graduation from Harvard, Button took off for Oslo, Norway, to defend his title at the 1952 Winter Olympics.

For the past year he had been thinking about creating a new jump that would wow the crowd and the judges. One thought kept coming back to him—a triple jump. Three complete, controlled revolutions in the air.

Nobody had ever done that before. Some believed it was impossible. It would be a quantum leap for skating, you might say.

Button worked on the triple for months. He would jump off his right foot going backwards, do three clockwise spins in the air before landing on his back right edge.

If that sounds complicated, it *is*.

Nobody in the world could do it. Dick Button couldn't do it. He was falling all over the ice. He was concentrating so hard on the triple that he forgot how to do single and double jumps. He was frustrated.

His mother and father, just like at the last Olympics, pleaded with Dick to quit the new jump and concentrate on what he already could do.

"At times in desperation I was almost ready to concede that the jump was beyond my achievement," said Button.

Dick practiced in private so none of his competitors would know what he was up to. At one of those practices just before the Olympics were to begin, something clicked. Button landed a triple. It was like an instant replay of the double axel before the 1948 Olympics.

About 30 seconds into his free skating program, Button had the feel of the ice and attempted the first triple jump in competition. He described it in his book *Dick Button on Skates*:

> I took the four-five-six preparation step and moved toward the edge into the loop. I forgot in momentary panic which shoulder should go forward and which back. I was extraordinarily conscious of the judges, who looked so immobile at rinkside. But this was it. The edge cut the ice and my arms lowered, shoulders turning against the rotation to allow a grip that would follow through. My knees closed as my feet crossed in the air. The wind cut my eyes, and the coldness caused tears to stream down my cheeks. Up! Up! Height was vital. Round and around again in a spin which took only a fraction of a second to complete before it landed on a clean steady back edge. I pulled away breathless, excited and overjoyed, as applause rolled from the faraway stands like the rumbling of a distant pounding sea.

For the second time, a gold medal was placed around his neck.

After the Olympics, Button gave up competitive skating

so he could attend Harvard Law School. He earned his degree in 1956, but the pull of skating wouldn't let go.

Button spent a short time skating in the Ice Capades, and in 1959 he began producing ice shows himself. He enjoyed being a producer and created several Broadway shows and the TV series *Battle of the Network Stars*. He has been a television skating analyst since 1962 and has won an Emmy award for his informative and entertaining commentary.

Dick Button was the United States Champion seven times, World Champion five times, and Olympic gold medalist twice. His "American Style" came to dominate skating over the next three decades, as the string of American champions on the following pages shows.

"There is a popular fallacy that falling down is the mark of a poor skater. But the truth is that when one stops falling, he has probably stopped improving."

—Dick Button

TENLEY ALBRIGHT

Tenley Albright didn't like to make mistakes, on or off the ice.

When she was 6 years old, her teacher found her in tears one day. The teacher asked what was wrong, and Tenley explained that she had written her name on a piece of paper but forgot to use a capital *A* for Albright. The teacher said that wasn't so terrible and told Tenley to throw the paper away and use another.

"No," sobbed Tenley. "It's wartime." (World War II was on and many things were in short supply.)

When her teacher suggested turning the paper over and writing on the other side, Tenley complained, "Then the mistake will just be on the other side."

Finally, the teacher gave Tenley an eraser, and the young girl rubbed out the small *a*.

"But I still made the mistake," she said mournfully.

This perfectionism would show up later in Tenley Albright's life, when she became the most accomplished female figure skater of her time.

Most skaters begin very young, but Tenley didn't get her first pair of skates until she was 9. Her father, a Boston surgeon, saw her enthusiasm for the sport and flooded the backyard of their house to form a tiny ice rink.

Two years later, in September of 1946, Tenley was struck by poliomyelitis—polio. It's caused by a virus that damages cells in the spinal cord. Polio doesn't kill, but it weakens muscles. We have vaccines today that prevent the disease, but when Tenley was a girl, there wasn't much that could be done.

Tenley spent three weeks in the hospital. When she got out, she needed to exercise to strengthen her back muscles. She decided to skate.

Tenley's back got stronger and her skating became smooth and powerful. Maribel Vinson, a well-known skating coach, spotted her and began giving her lessons. The young girl started to win local Boston competitions.

Early the next year, Tenley told Vinson that she'd like to go to Philadelphia and watch the Eastern Figure Skating Championships. "If you want to go," Vinson told the young girl, "go as a competitor."

*Tenley Albright. Her right leg is bandaged because she had
gashed her ankle in a recent training accident.*

Tenley took Vinson's challenge, and came home the Eastern Figure Skating Champion.

Other titles quickly followed. Tenley won the United
States Championship in 1952. The same year, she won a silver medal in the Olympics.

In 1953, she won the World Championship, becoming
the first American woman to claim that title. The competition was held outdoors in subzero temperatures at Davos,

Switzerland. Two British skaters collapsed on the ice due to the cold and high altitude.

After winning five consecutive United States Championships, Tenley was hungry for Olympic gold. She got it at the 1956 Winter Olympics in Cortina, Italy. She became the first in a long line of American female Olympic champions.

While she had been dominating the world as a skater, Tenley had been quietly attending Radcliffe College. She decided to follow in her father's footsteps and study medicine.

Her grades at Radcliffe were so good that Harvard Medical School offered to admit her after just three years of college. Shortly after she won the Olympic gold, Tenley retired from skating and entered medical school.

Today, nearly 40 years later, Tenley Albright (with a capital *A*) is a prominent surgeon in Boston. It makes sense that the little girl who hated to make mistakes would grow up and work in a field that leaves little room for errors.

"The one thing I want to be able to do after it's over is say that was my best. It's better to lose that way than to win with something less than that. But it's fun to win, isn't it?"
—*Tenley Albright*

CAROL HEISS

When Carol Heiss was 3 years old, she would climb on top of the fence surrounding her house and balance up there. Her mother didn't worry. She knew Carol would never fall off.

Carol was so good on her feet that her parents got her a pair of roller skates that year. When they were strapped on the little girl's feet for the first time, her mom and dad gently helped her up. They were about to take her by the hand, but she bolted away and skated around the basement as if she had been doing it for years.

For Christmas, Carol got a pair of ice skates.

Her mother took her to an ice rink and paid for a private lesson. The instructor took one look at Carol streaking across the ice, and he turned to Mrs. Heiss. "I can't teach the child anything," he told her. "Here's your money back."

Carol began to develop as a skater, and her family supported her. Every morning, the Heiss troupe would leave their Ozone Park, New York, house at 4:30 A.M. They'd drop Carol's father, Edward, off at the bakery where he worked. Her mother, Marie, would take Carol, her sister Nancy, and their brother Bruce to Madison Square Garden to skate before school.

As the children skated, Marie Heiss sat at rinkside with a portable drawing board, painting fabric designs, which she would sell to clothing companies.

All three Heiss children were good skaters, but Carol had the mark of a champion. Her biggest problem was that she was so small and light that her skates barely made a mark on the ice. When she traced her figures, judges had a difficult time telling if she had traced them properly.

Local skaters urged Marie Heiss to bring Carol to Pierre and Andree Brunet, the Olympic Pairs Champions and respected skating coaches.

The Brunets watched Carol skate, and decided the 6-year-old with the blond pigtails was so good they would coach her.

Under the Brunets' direction, Carol got even better. A week after Carol's tenth birthday, Carol and Nancy won the Middle Atlantic Ladies' Pairs Championship. At 11, Carol was the United States Novice Champion. At 13, she was the United States Junior Champion.

She entered the 1953 World Championships and finished fourth. Just 13 years old, and she was the fourth-best skater in the world!

At that same championship, an American named Hayes Alan Jenkins came in first among men. That name would become important later in Carol Heiss's life.

By 1954, Carol was in her prime. There was only one thing keeping her off the top step of the winners' stand—Tenley Albright. Five years older than Carol, Tenley was the United States Champion in 1952, 1953, and 1954. The two were set to meet in a showdown at the 1954 World Championships in Oslo, Norway.

It was New Year's Day and Carol was taking her final practice session. Her mother was at rinkside. Her sister, Nancy, was skating nearby. Both girls were deep in concentration, practicing their figures.

It all happened too quickly for Mrs. Heiss to react. Carol and Nancy were both skating backward toward each other. Neither girl saw the other. They crashed together, and the edge of Nancy's skate sliced into Carol's left leg just above the boot. Both girls toppled to the ground. Blood was all over Carol's leg and skate.

Carol tried to skate a few days later, but her leg collapsed under her. Doctors discovered that her muscles had been severed and her Achilles tendon damaged.

The World Championship was out of the question. Another girl was chosen to represent the United States in Oslo.

It was worse than that. The doctor also said, "Carol may never skate again."

Carol Heiss was miserable. Nancy Heiss felt almost as bad for having ruined her sister's chance of becoming World Champion.

Carol could have given up. Her leg was shattered, and she seemed destined to be Tenley Albright's runner-up for good.

But she didn't give up. Carol built up her left leg, and at the same time she learned how to jump off *either* leg. She came back in 1955 and was good enough to finish second in the World Championships—once again to Tenley Albright.

That April, Carol suffered another tragedy. Her mother was diagnosed with cancer. Marie Heiss didn't have long to live.

Carol was racing the clock. She was determined to win a World Championship while her mother was alive.

Tenley beat Carol again in the 1956 Olympics, winning the gold medal while Carol collected the silver. But three weeks later in the World Championships, Carol put on the performance of her life. All nine judges awarded her a 5.9 mark—nearly a perfect score. One judge was even seen *applauding*.

Tenley Albright had to settle for second place. Carol Heiss, just 16, was champion of the world. As always, her mother was at rinkside.

A few months later, Marie Heiss passed away. Carol would have to get the motivation to skate from inside.

She did. In 1957, she won the U.S. Championship, the North American Championship, and the World Champi-

Carol Heiss.

World Figure Skating Museum and Hall of Fame

onship. She did it again in 1958. She reeled off four straight U.S. Championships and five straight Worlds. Carol Heiss was the first woman to master the double axel. (A less impressive achievement was her appearance in the movie *Snow White and the Three Stooges*.)

All that was missing was an Olympic gold medal. She got that in 1960 at Squaw Valley, California, when all nine judges awarded her their first-place votes. Carol Heiss was undisputably the greatest female skater in the world.

A young skater named Hayes Alan Jenkins was mentioned earlier. He and Carol Heiss had a lot in common. Hayes also came from a skating family. Like Carol, he skated with his sister, and like Carol, his sister's name was Nancy. And like Carol, Hayes won an Olympic gold medal (in 1956).

Carol Heiss and Hayes Alan Jenkins have one more thing in common—they fell in love with each other and got married. They have three grown children and live in Akron, Ohio.

> *"The jumps were never supposed to mean so much. You need it all: the lightness and the airiness; the music, the personality. You need the caressing of the ice."*
>
> —Carol Heiss

AN AMERICAN TRAGEDY

It was Valentine's Day of 1961 and the United States Figure Skating team had gathered at Idlewild Airport (today called Kennedy) in New York City. The 18 skaters and 16 officials, coaches, and family members were heading for the

World Championships in Prague, Czechoslovakia.

Hopes and anticipation were high on Flight 548. The U.S. team was probably the best in the world. They were favored to win several medals.

The flight departed at 7:20 P.M. and flew all night across the Atlantic. The plane was due to refuel in Brussels, Belgium, and then continue on to Prague.

Just before 10:10 A.M., the Boeing 707 came into sight at Brussels. The sky was clear. The pilot was instructed to circle the airport twice to give another plane time to take off. He did that, then brought his plane down to 600 feet to approach the runway.

The landing gear was lowered, and then—for no apparent reason—raised again. The plane began to climb sharply.

The control tower tried to make contact with the pilot, but there was no response. Unusual engine sounds were heard on the ground. The plane began to shake and zigzag crazily. An emergency fire truck was immediately dispatched to the runway.

The Boeing 707 fell into a series of spins and then—horrifyingly—smashed into the ground near the village of Berg, four miles from the airport.

An enormous fireball soared high in the air. Explosions rocked the countryside. Pieces of the plane flew everywhere. A farmer working in his nearby field was killed by flying debris.

There were no survivors. The entire United States Figure Skating team had been instantly wiped out.

Skaters from all countries mourned the tragedy in Brus-

The victims of the most devastating accident in sports history.

sels. The World Championships were called off in memory of the Americans who would have been there.

Skating experts figured it would be a decade or more before young American skaters would rise up the ranks and rebuild a U.S. team that could compete on an international level. But just three years later, in the 1964 Olympics, the United States was back. Scott Ethan Allen won the bronze medal for men, and Vivian and Ronald Joseph won the bronze as a dance team.

And a young girl named Peggy Fleming placed sixth, showing the spark that would make her perhaps the most famous skater of all time.

PEGGY FLEMING

Peggy Gale Fleming was 12 years old when the plane crash killed the entire 1961 U.S. team. Her coach, Will Kipp, was one of the Americans killed in the crash.

Peggy had been born in San Jose, California. She was a shy girl. Her mother thought figure skating might help her become more outgoing. It was obvious from the start that she had something other skaters lacked.

Just 15 in 1964, Fleming won the United States Championship and made a strong showing in the Olympics. For Peggy to reach the top, she and her parents felt she should train with Carlo Fassi, the former champion of Italy and two-time Olympian.

In 1965 the whole Fleming family—mom, dad, and three daughters—moved from Pasadena, California, to Colorado Springs so Peggy could work with Fassi.

Shortly after the move, Peggy's father, a newspaper pressman, died of a heart attack. To cope with her grief, Peggy submerged herself in her skating and her studies.

She would get up at dawn to skate for a few hours, take her regular classes at Colorado College, and then put in another several hours on the ice. She even found time to coach the college hockey team, the Red Barons.

With her talent and Fassi's coaching, by 1968 Peggy Fleming had won five national championships and two world titles.

There was something about Peggy Fleming that seemed to separate her from all other skaters. She was cool on the ice. Nothing seemed to rattle her.

The other skaters would attack the ice, fighting to execute their jumps and spins. They had "linebacker legs"—muscular thighs they used to propel them into the air.

Peggy was small and fragile—5'4" and 109 pounds. One magazine said she resembled Bambi. She didn't rocket her way around the ice. She glided, effortlessly. She looked like a ballerina. It looked as though she barely touched the ice.

"She is the one without the bruises," reported *Sports Illustrated.*

At the same time, she was an average American girl. Peggy loved banana cream pie and the Jefferson Airplane. She would buy six cans of hair spray at a time to keep every strand in place.

She would wrap Saran Wrap around her legs to help sweat off extra pounds. If a restaurant didn't have her favorite dish—macaroni and cheese—she would go back to her hotel room and whip up a batch herself.

When the 1968 Olympics rolled around, Peggy Fleming was 19. She had practiced 20,000 hours over the past ten years. And she was favored and ready to take skating's highest crown.

"I've worked all these years for this one thing," she said. "But it wouldn't be the end of the world if I lost."

At the opening ceremonies in Grenoble, France, 50,000 paper roses were dropped from a plane. A group of parachutists followed, and they landed in the Olympic rings.

Peggy stayed with her mother in a hotel across the street from the Grenoble railroad station. Doris Fleming spent the nights before the skating competition sewing six costumes for Peggy. Eventually they agreed on a chartreuse outfit with chiffon and rhinestones.

As Peggy stepped out on the ice at the Stade de Glace, the rhinestones in her sleeve got caught on her beige tights. She was afraid the entire costume was going to rip.

It didn't. She skated flawlessly. At the end of the compulsory figures—which made up 60 percent of the total score in those days—she had a 77-point lead over the next skater. Thirty-one other skaters were even further behind.

She could have taken it easy, performed a casual free skate, and cruised to a gold medal. But she didn't. The strains of Tchaikovsky filled the arena and Peggy put all her talent, grace, and style into the next 4 minutes and 9 seconds.

"I was like in a fog when I went out for the final program," she said later. "I didn't really hear the audience; the music was the only friend I could cling to."

Peggy didn't feel that she had done her best, and she burst into tears at the finish. But to the crowd and the judges, it was a dazzling performance. When the scores were calculated, Peggy had an 88-point lead over Gaby Seyfert of East Germany.

It would be the only gold medal the United States would win at the 1968 Olympics.

*Peggy Fleming after charming the world at the
1968 Olympics in Grenoble, France.*

This was the first time the Olympics were broad-
cast around the world, live via satellite. Within a week,
Peggy Fleming went from being an ordinary American
young woman to a worldwide celebrity and symbol of figure
skating.

She was invited to the White House twice. She starred in
seven TV specials, performed in the Ice Follies and Holiday
on Ice.

Peggy got married and took ten years off to raise her two

sons. In recent years she has come back to skating, performing professionally and doing television commentary with Dick Button during the Olympic Games.

"I wish I could have done the real, real difficult jumps, but times were different."

—*Peggy Fleming*

DOROTHY HAMILL

While nothing seemed to bother Peggy Fleming before a competition, Dorothy Hamill was a bundle of nerves. You would think that the greatest skaters in the world would be brimming with self-confidence and able to handle any pressure situation. In reality, they are often plagued by the same nervousness and self-doubt the rest of us experience.

"It's like going to an execution—" Dorothy Hamill once said of her competitions—"your own. I stand there in the dressing room thinking, 'Am I going to fall? Why am I doing this? I'll never do it again.'"

Dorothy suffered from a horrible case of stage fright before each performance. At the 1974 World Championships in Munich, she was waiting at the edge of the ice to be introduced for her free skating program. The marks for the previous skater were flashed on the scoreboard, and they were low. The crowd began to boo and jeer.

Thinking the crowd's anger was directed toward her, Dorothy broke down in tears and ran off the ice into her father's arms.

This, from a young woman who would win the U.S. Championship three years in a row, the World Championship once, and an Olympic gold medal.

Getting ready to skate may have been hard, but on the ice Dorothy Hamill made everything look easy. Other skaters would build up a head of steam, racing halfway across the rink to launch their jumps. Dorothy didn't seem to need this preparation. She would jump effortlessly and hang in the air longer than gravity allowed mere mortals. When she did her delayed axel, it seemed as if she stopped in the air before completing the one and a half revolutions. She looked as if she was taking her time.

Dorothy was inspired by her idol, ballet dancer Mikhail Baryshnikov. And she was motivated by Carlo Fassi, the same coach who helped Peggy Fleming achieve greatness.

The night before the Olympic free skate in 1976, Dorothy couldn't sleep. She had fallen down in her final warm-up, and that had shaken her already fragile confidence. More than a half a billion people around the world would be watching the next day on television.

Dorothy Hamill was 19, and she was nervous.

But she knew what she had to do when she skated onto the ice in her pink dress at the Olympic Ice Hall in Innsbruck, Austria. The music began and she did the program she had rehearsed hundreds of times: delayed axel, walley jump, double axel, double toe loop, camel spin, double lutz into a back spiral, double axel, double salchow, split, double toe loop, butterfly, layback spin, delayed double salchow, Bauer spiral into a double lutz, walley, split, split. She finished the performance with her signature, the "Hamill camel" (a camel spin into a sit spin).

Bouquets of daffodils, tulips, and roses rained down on the ice. Dorothy, who is nearsighted, squinted up to see her marks. For technical merit, eight judges had given her a 5.8 and one a 5.9. For artistic interpretation, it was 5.9 right across the board.

She didn't have to worry about the crowd jeering. A roar went up in the Olympic Ice Hall. Dorothy Hamill had won the gold.

After the Olympics, Dorothy received a hero's welcome in her hometown of Riverside, Connecticut. Thousands of people lined the streets to greet her. A plaque was dedicated at the little pond where she had taken her first hesitant steps on a pair of $5.95 ice skates so many years before.

Dorothy Hamill's "wedge" haircut inspired a full-fledged fashion craze in the late 1970s. A few months after the Olympics, she was in a museum with her mother when a man said to her, "I like your Dorothy Hamill haircut."

She didn't bother telling him she *was* Dorothy Hamill.

When you're just 19 and your childhood dream has already come true, you have to find *another* dream. The 50-year-old Ice Capades went bankrupt in 1991, so Dorothy Hamill—the president of Dorothy Hamill International—bought the show.

She had skated in the Ice Capades after the Olympics and always had a warm place in her heart for it. Dorothy and the company put on an ice version of *Cinderella*, saving the Ice Capades from financial ruin.

Dorothy was briefly married to Dean Paul Martin, son of the entertainer Dean Martin. Today she is married to Ken-

Dorothy Hamill.

neth Forsythe, a doctor of sports medicine and a former member of the Canadian Olympic ski team. They live in California with their daughter Alexandra. Dorothy sold the Ice Capades and retired from professional skating at the end of 1994.

> *"You're skating and doing the most difficult things, and the audience is with you. They're clapping, cheering. You're floating. It's like nothing else I've ever felt."*
>
> —*Dorothy Hamill*

JOHN CURRY

Three days before Dorothy Hamill won her gold medal at Innsbruck, Englishman John Curry won the men's gold medal.

Unlike Hamill and many of the other skaters in this book, John Curry didn't live a storybook life. He didn't have a wealthy, supportive family to help him achieve his goals. His father disapproved of John's early passion for dance, and refused to let him take lessons. Only grudgingly did he let his son pursue skating. The elder Curry hoped it would just be a passing phase.

John was miserable at home in Birmingham, England, and used skating as his escape. "I rather dreaded going home," he said. "At the rink I was in an environment where I could forget completely everything else. In skating I was happy."

Having only seen his son skate twice, John's father died of tuberculosis when John was 16 years old.

After his father died, John made the decision to pursue skating as a career. He went to London to study the art, paying his bills by working in a supermarket and as a receptionist. Most of his bills, anyway.

"There was never a shilling for the gas meter, and stepping out of bed onto a cold floor, then washing in the cold, then going to a cold ice-rink at six in the morning all seemed unrelievedly horrible. But skating exercised its hold over me."

John Curry didn't have the classic fresh-scrubbed looks you see in other skaters. He was very thin, and he had his hair curled to make himself look more cheerful and healthy.

He didn't look like an athlete. He could run faster and jump higher than other young men, but he wasn't good at sports. Making things tougher for him, John was gay and never made any effort to hide it.

John Curry didn't even like the cold, which would seem to be a requirement for someone pursuing a career as an ice skater.

He wasn't a child prodigy. He was slow to develop as a skater, suffering through years of failure. During one competition in London, he fell down six times in 3 minutes. Skating judges looked down on the experimental moves he enjoyed performing.

Somehow he managed to finish fourth in the 1972 World Championships. But the next year he came in seventh and the judges advised him to consider another career. At age 23, they told him, he was too old to make a major improvement in his skating. He thought seriously about giving up skating and starting all over again as a dancer.

The turning point came when someone advised John to seek out two top coaches—Gustave Lussi, who had coached Dick Button and was an expert in jumping; and Carlo Fassi, who coached Peggy Fleming and Dorothy Hamill, and who specialized in helping skaters trace their figures. Both men saw something in Curry and agreed to work with him.

Lussi had a theory that skaters rely too much on momentum to jump, when they *should* be using their muscles. He had Curry practice jumps in a tiny room where it would be impossible to build up momentum.

John unlearned everything he had been taught. It was

John Curry.

grueling work, and he fell 30 to 40 times a day. But after three weeks, Lussi's lessons began to sink in. Using muscle instead of momentum, John's jumps became higher, longer, and smoother.

Curry spent the next weeks with Carlo Fassi. Once again, he made remarkable improvement in his skating. He also went through psychological training to help calm his nerves before a performance and to visualize a perfect routine.

"For perhaps the first and only time in my life," he would later write, "skating was absolutely easy for me."

John's confidence improved along with his technique, and he came in third in the 1975 World Championships. He went into the 1976 Winter Olympics feeling he had a good shot at the gold. At the opening ceremonies, he was chosen to carry the British flag.

After the compulsory figures, Curry was in second place. As he stepped on the ice to begin his free-skating performance, he said to himself: "The next five minutes are going to determine the rest of your life."

And for the first time in his life, everything came together—his form, his technique, his mental outlook. As he landed his last triple jump perfectly, he thought, "You've just won the Olympics, kid!"

Most skaters, after winning a gold medal, hit the ice-show circuit. That's the usual route, and it's tempting. Having struggled financially his whole life, John received offers that would enable him to make enough money in two years to be set for life.

But Curry *hated* ice shows. He felt they demeaned the artistry of skating. "I never could see the point of spending 12 years training to go dress up in a Bugs Bunny suit," he told one interviewer.

Instead of grabbing the cash, Curry went for the freedom. He formed the John Curry Skating Company with the intention of taking skating to an entirely new level.

World-renowned choreographers such as Twyla Tharp and Peter Martins were brought in to create his routines. Original music was commissioned to accompany them. Spectacular costumes were designed.

Curry didn't just incorporate dance and ballet into skating; he performed actual ballets on ice and created new ones. In one piece he performed a balletic version of the fable *Icarus*, wearing enormous wings so he could skate too close to the sun. He took his show to Broadway in 1977 and around the world in the following years.

Curry threw off everyone's expectations of what ice shows were supposed to be. There were no hummable show tunes. No animal costumes to charm the kids. Often there was no humor. And often, hisses and boos could be heard from the crowd. Some people clearly expected—and would have preferred—Bugs Bunny on ice.

"I have to be honest and admit that giving other people pleasure is not the motivating force," Curry said. "I do not accept such an idea. I skate because I love skating, myself."

Some of his ice ballets were hailed as brilliant and innovative. Others failed to capture the imagination of critics or audiences. But Curry continued to pursue his vision of what skating could be—not just a sport and a popular entertainment, but also an art form. His creativity would inspire the skaters of the 1980s, 1990s, and beyond.

Tragically, John Curry did not live to see the effect of his pioneering work. He died of AIDS in April of 1994 at the age of 44.

"There are only certain times in my life when I feel any kind of real unity or completeness or peace: these times are when I am skating. The ice, then, is home."

—John Curry

4

⤸⊗⤸

A Day in the Life of a Young Skater:
Tara Lipinski

Figure skating is probably the most difficult, demanding, competitive, and exhausting sport in the world. Athletes in other sports usually don't show their potential until the end of high school, and then the best get coddled through college or minor leagues until they reach the top.

Figure skaters usually start when they are barely out of diapers, and then they quickly enter a world that's very different from a "normal" childhood—a world filled with coaches, choreographers, ballet lessons, tutors, traveling, competitions, and countless hours of practice.

A young skater has to pass a series of tests required by the United States Figure Skating Association as she makes her way from Novice to Junior to Senior. If she's gifted, injury-free, and works diligently for about ten years, and luck is with her, she has a chance—a *small* chance—to win medals, fame, and millions of dollars.

She *really* needs the money at the *start*. A good coach costs about $50 per hour, and choreographers between $5,000 and $10,000 per year. Private rink-time goes for $100 to $250 per hour. Then there's equipment, sharpening, costumes, music, traveling expenses, and entry fees. Her parents have to count on spending at least $25,000 a year to pay for it all, and probably closer to $50,000.

Some skaters get grants; others are sponsored by wealthy patrons. Usually it's mom and dad digging deep into their savings accounts and using money they had set aside for college.

But if the skater comes home with an Olympic medal, she'll get all that back and much more.

Tara Lipinski is a very promising 13-year-old girl (born June 10, 1982) whom you should be hearing a lot about in the next few years. When she was just 3, Tara took up roller skating, and she became so good at it that she won the freestyle event in the United States Nationals in 1991. She began ice skating when she was 6 and found that she liked it even more than roller skating.

Tara placed fourth in the 1995 World Juniors Championship. She has been featured on *Good Morning America* and in *The New York Times*. Tara dreams of making the United States team for the 1998 or 2002 Olympics. "Oh, I would love that!" she gushes. Her ultimate goal: "To win the Olympics."

Tara was born in Philadelphia, Pennsylvania and raised in Sewell, New Jersey, where she learned how to skate. Her dad, Jack, works for an oil company and her mom, Pat, is a homemaker.

A few years ago Jack was promoted and transferred to Houston, Texas. The family moved west, but there are no high-level skating facilities or coaches in Houston. Tara was showing the potential to become a great skater, so the Lipinskis made a painful decision—Tara and her mother would move to Delaware so Tara could train, while her father

A Day in the Life of a Young Skater: Tara Lipinski

would stay in Texas and come east to be with the family as frequently as possible.

"What do you do when you have a kid who wants to do something so terribly badly?" asks Tara's dad. Her mother says, "She's happy, and when this is over, we can say we did what we thought was right. She can't imagine her life without skating."

John Everett

The arrangement is difficult, but it seems to be working out. Jack Lipinski flies to Delaware every two or three weeks, and Tara and her mom spend their summers and holidays in Texas.

Here's a typical day in the life of Tara Lipinski.

7:00 A.M.: Wake up and warm up with stretching exercises. Breakfast is usually a bagel with butter, orange juice, and a vitamin. "I can pretty much eat anything," says Tara, who weighs 69 pounds. Many other skaters have to follow a strict diet to keep their weight down.

8:00–12:00: Mrs. Keller, her teacher, comes to Tara's home. Tara went to a regular school through the fifth grade, and then switched to private tutoring. "It was hard to get all my skating in and go to school at the same time," she says. Mrs. Keller teaches Tara in all subjects, and gives her homework, too. Tara's favorite subjects are science, math, and reading. Her least favorite is English.

12:00 P.M.: Tara's mother drives her to the ice rink at the University of Delaware in Newark, Delaware. Tara doesn't have the whole rink to herself, but she works one-on-one with her coach, Jeff DiGregorio.

Tara spends most of the time working on jumps. She can land the triple loop, triple toe loop, and triple salchow. In 1995 she conquered two jumps very few skaters have mastered—the triple lutz and triple flip. Tara can't do a triple axel yet (she *can* do double axels), but plans to begin working on that "king of jumps" very soon. "I like to jump, and do all the revolutions," she says. "I think it's a lot of fun."

A Day in the Life of a Young Skater: Tara Lipinski

Tara's favorite skaters are Oksana Baiul, Kurt Browning, and Todd Eldredge. She has met them all. In fact, last year she performed in an exhibition with Oksana. The skater Tara would most like to meet is Elvis Stojko.

During practice, Tara wears tights and a practice dress with a turtleneck sweater over it. For competitions, she wears more elaborate costumes made by a Delaware woman named Lee LeFrank. Tara has two competition outfits, one blueish green and the other black. She doesn't wear makeup in practice, but she will put on some rouge and lipstick for a competition. She owns just one pair of skates and has them sharpened every two and a half weeks.

12:40: Tara takes a 20-minute break. She usually spends the time talking with her friends, fellow skaters Laura, Kylene, Tina, and Chrisha. When asked if any of her skating friends are boys, she replies, "There aren't a lot of boy skaters." Tara's best friend off the ice is Tara Brooks, who used to live across the street from her in Texas but now lives in California.

1:00: Another session with Jeff DiGregorio. This time they will concentrate on Tara's spins. She likes doing spins almost as much as she does jumps, and has done 20 to 25 rotations in a single spin.

1:40: Tara takes a quick break to tie her skates. They tend to become loose after a session on the ice.

1:50: Another practice session. Tara skates by herself now, practicing the moves she and Jeff worked on in the morning.

2:30: Lunchtime. Tara usually has spaghetti with marinara sauce, which she purchases from a snack bar at the rink.

3:00: Tara and her friends turn a few cartwheels to warm up. Then she goes out on the ice for a lesson with her choreographer, Jill Cosgrove. Jill and Tara work on footwork, in-between steps, arm and head movements, and other elements of her program.

Even though she loves jumping and spinning, Tara realizes the importance of choreography. Once, during a roller skating competition, she forgot her whole program and had to improvise a new one on the spot.

3:40: Tara gets a snack—some Reese's Pieces—and something to drink.

4:20: One last freestyle practice session, with coach Ron Luddington. Ron and his wife, Nancy, were the United States Pairs Champions from 1957 to 1960, and they won the bronze medal in the 1960 Olympics.

Tara with her best friend, Tara Brooks, in Sugarland, Texas.

A Day in the Life of a Young Skater: Tara Lipinski

Then Tara is done skating for the day. Altogether, she spent about four hours on the ice. When asked if she ever gets sick of skating, she replies without hesitation, "No, never."

5:00: Tara goes up to the ballet room at the rink, where she has a lesson with her ballet coach, Sergei, who is from Russia.

6:00: Tara's mom drives her home. Tara loves to cook, and after she finishes her homework she'll help her mom make dinner. Usually they make pudding or Jell-O for dessert.

7:30: Tara relaxes with some TV or a board game. Her favorite shows include: *The Nanny, Home Improvement,* and *Grace Under Fire.* Her favorite games are Taboo, Crack the Case, Clue, and Monopoly.

She will also play with her dog Mischi (short for "mischief"). Her other dogs—Brandy, Lancy (Lancelot), and Cammy (Camelot)—are in Texas with her dad. On those rare days when she's not in training, Tara loves to play tennis.

10:00: Bedtime.

5

⌦

Fancy Footwork:
When You Watch Skating on TV

With any sport, fans can sit back and enjoy the performance, or they can appreciate the skill of the athletes on a deeper level. That's certainly true with skating. On TV you'll hear the commentators talk about jumps, spins, scoring, costumes, music, and other aspects of the sport. In this chapter, these things are explained so you can have a better understanding of what you're seeing.

SPINNING

One of the most beautiful things skaters do is spin. It looks impossible. Ordinary people can hardly do it at all, and only the best skaters in the world can do it effortlessly.

A top skater can complete as many as 6 rotations in 1 second, and 70 in a single spin. In order to advance through the ranks of amateur skating, young skaters are required to make 7 rotations to pass a proficiency test. For some reason, left-handed skaters usually spin clockwise, while right-handed skaters spin counterclockwise. Women usually do more spins than men, though Scott Davis is one of the best spinners around.

When they spin, good skaters look at eye level at all times and keep their body very straight. They don't want to slide forward while they're spinning. The object is to spin in one place.

Sometimes they spin on one pointed toe. This is called a "scratch spin," and they can do it so rapidly they look like a blur. Other times they'll spin more slowly, with the bottom of the blade flat on the ice. In either case, the leg on the ice is kept very straight.

While she is spinning, the skater can do any number of things to make the spin more interesting. She may lean her head and shoulders backward and arch her back. This is called a "layback" or "headback spin." She may put her free foot down the outside of her skating foot. This is called the "corkscrew spin."

A "parallel" or "arabesque" spin is when she leans forward, arches her back, and holds her free leg behind her, parallel to the ice. Her body looks like the letter T. This is also called a "camel spin." If she's in a camel and reaches back to hold her nonskating foot in her hand, it's a "grab-hold spin." You may also see a "flying camel," where the skater appears to be leaping over a barrel before she begins to spin.

When you see a skater start a spin and then sink down and extend one foot in front of her, that's a "sit spin." Skaters call it "shooting the duck." If she extends her foot to the side or behind, it's a "broken leg spin." If she leaps in the air first and takes a sitting position before landing, it's a "flying sit spin."

The skater can speed up or slow down her spin simply by moving her arms. If she gradually pulls her arms close to her body, the centrifugal force is reduced and she spins like a top.

You're probably wondering why skaters don't get dizzy.

They often do—the first few times they try a new spin or position. But after executing it a few times, most skaters aren't bothered by the spinning sensation.

There are a few things skaters do to prevent dizziness. One technique is called "spotting." Every time they turn around, they try to fix their eyes on a single spot somewhere in the rink. This gives their brain a momentary stable image to focus on so it can recover its equilibrium. In practice, skaters who feel dizzy will sometimes put a finger a few inches away from their eyes and stare at the finger to take the dizziness away. But people who become very dizzy when spinning in circles usually look for a line of work other than skating.

It's very dramatic when a skater finishes her performance with a spin. You'll see that she will extend her arms to slow herself down and then lightly touch the ice with her other leg. Some skaters like to end very suddenly by stabbing the ice with the point of their free toe. Philipe Candeloro of France will sometimes end a performance by sitting right down and spinning on the ice until he stops turning.

"If you get perfectly on the ball of one foot with just one and a half inches of the skate blade touching the ice," says Olympic gold medal winner Scott Hamilton, "you can spin for days."

JUMPS

As soon as most skaters master their basic turns, they usually want to learn how to do jumps—especially the men. These are considered the most exciting move in figure skating.

"There's so much power involved," says four-time World Champion Kurt Browning. "Not raw, unfocused power, but pointed, purposeful force. The intensity is amazing. You can feel every muscle waiting and waiting. Then, if you put them into action at the right moment, you explode. It's a great feeling."

Every jump consists of five parts: the run-in, takeoff, rotation in the air, landing, and landing curve.

During the run-in, the skater gains the speed she'll need to perform the jump. Her skating leg is like a spring. You'll notice she will bend her knee deeply and push off that leg hard. This is so she can get as high off the ice as possible. Height is crucial in jumping, because it gives the skater more time to complete her rotations in the air. As you might expect, skaters need very strong leg muscles.

On some jumps, such as the salchow, she takes off from the edge of her skate. On others, such as the lutz, she pushes off from her toe. Skaters don't jump around in a circle. They jump *up*, and then rotate in the air. So most of the rotation takes place on the way down. It's crucial that the skater pull her arms close to her chest to achieve the most spin in the air. The body and head should be vertical.

Coming back to the ice, the skater will extend her arms for balance and her free leg behind. If she lands the jump cleanly, she will land on one foot. She'll try to land on the front part of the blade while moving backwards. If you hear a scraping noise, that means she landed on the flat of the blade.

The landing should be soft, with the knee bent. Once she is down, she will straighten the leg and move on to the next part of her performance.

To do a double jump, she has to complete *two* rotations in the air. For a triple jump, it's *three*. Naturally, the skater has to get higher in the air and have perfect form to land these jumps cleanly.

There's no doubt that skaters fall more than they did ten or twenty years ago. This isn't because today's skaters aren't as good as those from the past. It's because today's skaters are attempting much more difficult jumps. Even the best in the world can't land them cleanly every time.

"When there weren't as many triple jumps in the programs," says Nancy Kerrigan, "you didn't see as many falls or mistakes."

When you see somebody fall at the end of a double or triple jump, it's not that they can't do it. They probably did the same jump flawlessly over and over again during training. Usually, they fall because they are overanxious. They're concerned about getting all the rotations in, so they start rotating too early and their form is thrown off.

Some critics argue that figure skating has turned into one big jumping contest in the last few years. Winners, they believe, are the skaters who can pull off the most spectacular leaps, and nothing else really matters. It's true that jumps have become more frequent, more challenging, and more important. Hopefully, there will always be room for skaters who show style, grace, and beauty on the ice.

The United States Figure Skating Association rulebook lists 47 jumps. It's impossible to describe them all, but three popular jumps are described in detail in the following sections. The differences between them are sometimes subtle. Even after reading about them, you may have a hard time telling one from the other. Watching them in slow motion helps.

THE AXEL

This is the easiest jump to recognize, because it's one of the few which the skater runs into *forward*. Just before take-off, she bends her left leg and swings her arms way back. As she launches off her left outside edge, both arms are waist high and begin to rise. They will reach the top of her head at the jump's highest point.

As the left leg straightens out and thrusts down, the right one opens and bends. The legs are not together again until the skater descends.

There is a great temptation for the skater to begin turning as soon as she is off the ice. Skaters are always advised to get the height first and *then* begin the rotation. "Rotation is the least of your worries," according to two-time Olympic gold medalist Dick Button.

International Skating Union

The axel jump.

After one revolution, the skater is on the way down, the arms back to waist level. There is still a half revolution to go, and the skater ends up backward on her right foot. Her left leg extends back and her arms reach out at shoulder height.

The axel is beautiful to watch. It can remind you of a long jumper. The skater flies higher and farther than in any other jump. In fact, 1980 Olympic Champion Robin Cousins of England holds the record for the longest jump, a 19'1" axel. Axels are almost always performed in the center of the rink, because they require so much room.

Most amazingly, when Norway's Axel Paulsen landed the first axel in 1882, he did it while wearing *speed* skates!

THE SALCHOW

This jump is also named after its inventor, Ulrich Salchow of Sweden. After a forward run-in, the skater turns around to skate backward. Her arms begin to lower, her right leg extends behind. There is a very wide leg swing. The right leg comes forward and at the same time the left knee bends.

The skater then pushes off her left foot to get into the air. The arms come up to shoulder height and she turns counterclockwise in the air, making one revolution. The arms then

International Skatir

The salchow jump.

come down and she lands on her right foot, skating backward again. The left leg is extended back to finish gracefully.

THE LUTZ

Alois Lutz never achieved much fame as a skater, as Axel Paulsen and Ulrich Salchow did. But the lutz jump was named after this young man from Vienna, who created it in 1918.

Skating backward on a wide curve, the skater reaches forward with her left arm and slightly back with her right. Similarly, the left leg is deeply bent and the right one extends back in the air. She takes off on the back outside edge of the left skate, with the assist of her toe pick.

As she takes off, her two arms switch position, the right one moving forward. Both arms come up, about eye-high.

Up in the air, both legs straighten. There is one rotation (in the opposite direction of the curve), and her arms come down in the middle. The left knee bends and the right one stays extended until the backward landing, when it bends to cushion the impact. Finally, the left leg comes back for a graceful finish.

International Skating Union

The lutz jump.

If you watch Scott Hamilton skate, you'll notice that he always starts off his program with a lutz jump in the corner of the rink.

There are plenty of variations on all these jumps: the delayed axel, toe salchow, half toe split salchow, half split lutz, inside lutz (also called a "toe walley"), one foot lutz, and so on. It's up to the skater's inventiveness to use the unlimited possibilities and create a program that will satisfy the judges and amaze the crowd.

QUADS AND QUINTS

When Axel Paulsen pulled off the first axel, it was like Roger Bannister's breaking the 4-minute mile and Chuck Yeager's breaking the sound barrier. No skater had ever done more than one rotation in the air before, so people believed it couldn't be done. Paulsen opened up all kinds of possibilities that are still being explored today.

A few skaters (Karl Schafer of Austria, Gillis Grafstrom of Sweden) were doing double jumps (two rotations) in the late 1920s, but not in competition. You didn't see flying spins or jump combinations back then.

Skaters did lots of spirals and slow spins. They skated *slower*. They didn't have rock and roll to skate to. It wasn't until after World War II that skaters were doing double jumps and triple jumps.

Today, triple jumps have become commonplace, and a few skaters are turning *four* times in the air! Brian Boitano, the

1986 World Champion, was nailing quadruple jumps during practice in 1987. He tried a quad toe loop in the World Championships that year and fell.

"I sacrificed my world title for it," Boitano said afterward of the quad. "I won't sacrifice an Olympic medal." He didn't, winning the gold in the 1988 Olympics.

The same year, at the World Championships in Budapest, Canada's Kurt Browning completed a quadruple jump in competition for the first time. His body flew 12 feet across the ice in .8 seconds, spinning the equivalent of 300 revolutions per minute.

"The feeling of a perfectly executed quad is something only a few people in the world know," says Browning, "but it's not the physical sensation that matters as much as the satisfaction you feel—unleashing so much power and yet sustaining control."

Now that they're doing quads, it makes one wonder how high can a human being jump? How long can a skater stay in the air, and how many revolutions can he or she make in that amount of time?

"I think there'll probably be a quintuple jump—a quint— five revolutions in full flight," says Browning, who believes quadruple jumps will soon be commonplace. "I don't think I'll be the first one to land it, but every day, I see kids who spin so fast it makes me dizzy. One of them will make it."

Then we'll *really* be seeing a lot of skaters with their backsides on the ice.

BACKFLIPS

During exhibitions, you'll often see somebody leap up with both feet, do a backward somersault in the air, and land on their skates. It never fails to drive a crowd crazy. 1976 U.S. Champion Terry Kubicka was the first—and last skater to do a backflip in the Olympics. After that, the trick was banned. Skating officials decided they were too dangerous.

During a practice session for the 1994 Olympics, Surya Bonaly of France did a backflip just a few yards from Japan's Midori Ito. Many skating experts viewed Bonaly's stunt as an attempt to intimidate Ito, who was a favorite. It may have worked. Ito fell out of medal contention. But so did Bonaly.

PRESENTATION

Skating is show business, and skaters put a tremendous amount of effort into putting on a good show. A few jumps and spins alone won't fill a 4-minute program, and it won't win any medals either. It's the in-between steps, gestures, and head movements that make the difference between champions and tenth place.

It may take weeks or even months for a skater to put together a program. The British team of Torvill and Dean have been known to spend days on a 10-second portion of their program. Other skaters will slap an entire routine together in four hours. But *all* top skaters rehearse hundreds of times before using a program in a competition.

There is very little improvisation among skaters. Once they perfect their program, they rarely change it. Some-

Charlotte.

One of the first indoor ice rinks, the Prince's Skating Club in London. Skaters would dance to music from a live orchestra. The 1908 Olympic figure skating events were held here.

Brasseur and Eisler.

Scott Davis.

Natalia Mishkutenok and Artur Dmitriev of Russia, who won the gold medal for pairs at the 1992 Olympics and the silver in 1994.

Viktor Petrenko.

Nancy Kerrigan provin she's an athlete as well a an artist.

Paul Harvath

Michelle Kwan doing a layback spin.

Jim Graves, IceSport Press

Elvis Stojko.

Peggy Fleming was still thrilling fans years after her Olympic medals.

times, however, if a skater knows she needs another point or two to win, she will throw in an extra jump at the end of her performance. Oksana Baiul did that in the 1994 Olympics, and it worked. She beat Nancy Kerrigan by an eyelash.

Skaters don't usually create their programs by themselves. Their choreographers do it for them. Robin Cousins and Torvill and Dean are exceptions. Some choreographers even draw a map of the program for the skater. Each jump, spin, and step is written out on paper.

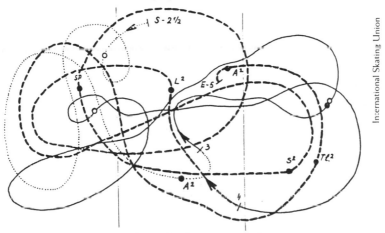

A "road map" of one of John Curry's performances.

The top skaters, you notice, use the entire rink. They don't do all the elements of their performance in one area. They don't usually do jumps near the edge of the ice, because some spectators won't see them over there.

These days, Olympic-quality skaters put on a show with 10 to 15 jumps, 2 to 4 spins, and all the steps that connect them.

Jumps are exhausting. It's no coincidence that the most energetic leaps are often followed by slow, balletic movements—the skater uses those moments to catch her breath.

Skaters usually do their toughest jump near the beginning of the program, when they have the most energy.

But they don't want to pack *all* their best moves at the beginning and leave a flat ending. They try to pace the performance so they won't be too winded at any one point. The idea is to start with a bang, finish with a flourish, and make sure nobody gets bored in the middle.

A skater wants to display her versatility, keep the crowd guessing and anxious for more. If she can get them clapping, laughing, or even crying, that's great. It's very difficult to wow a crowd and please a judge at the same time.

Finally, a great skater will end her performance at precisely the final note of music with a dramatic gesture. Torvill and Dean "died" on the ice to finish their classic performance of *Bolero*. The team was awarded straight 6.0s from the judges.

For the next couple of years, skaters were dying all over the ice.

COSTUMES

"Tasteful selection of sportswear is essential and use of vulgar or gaudy 'carnival' costume is inappropriate."
—A History and Annotated Bibliography
of Skating Costume, 1970

First of all, they aren't called "costumes." For ladies, they are officially called "dresses." For men, they are "outfits." But for the sake of simplicity, we'll call them costumes here.

When figure skating competitions were first held in the 1800s, they took place outdoors on natural ice. The purpose of a costume back then wasn't to make a skater look good or feel comfortable; it was simply to keep her *warm*. She just wore her usual winter clothes—heavy skirts down to the feet, hoops, bustle, and corset. Men would compete wearing jacket, scarf, tie, and gloves. Both sexes wore hats. Obviously, it was difficult to be very athletic on the ice when they were wearing so much clothing.

Hemlines rose to the knees around World War I, and so did skating costumes. Sonja Henie was the first to skate in a knee-length skirt. Even though she was only 11 years old when she competed in the 1924 Olympics, her costume was considered shocking. But other skaters saw how her skirt gave her more freedom of movement, and they followed her lead.

Gradually, female skaters began wearing more elaborate costumes, with fancy fabrics, beads, fur, special designs and decorations. The men were slower to change. Until recent years, the usual uniform for men was a short black or navy blue tuxedo. In the 1950s, Dick Button showed up on the ice wearing a *white* jacket, and that was big news.

Color TV and lightweight synthetic fabrics came along during the 1960s, and skaters of both sexes took advantage of them. You started seeing wild colors and skin-tight costumes that displayed the skater's body more. Men began wearing one-piece jump suits. Gary Beacom skated while he was wrapped from head to toe in black nylon, and wearing skates on his *hands*. Christopher Bowman wore all black and dyed his hair black to match. Women were seen with bare midriffs and bikini tops.

Frantic activity in the makeup room before the 1991 U.S. Championships.

Things were starting to get out of hand. The International Skating Union became concerned that costumes were detracting from the athletic nature of skating. After the 1988 Olympics, they passed guidelines that limited how outrageous skating costumes could be. If a skater broke those rules in competition, she was subject to a .1 or .2 deduction from her marks.

A spectacular costume doesn't make a better skater, but it doesn't hurt. Today, costumes for the top skaters are custom designed and handmade. Depending on the fabric and amount of decoration, they can cost as much as $2,500. And most skaters always keep a spare costume ready, in case their costume rips.

During the 1994 Olympics, Nancy Kerrigan wore a Vera Wang outfit with 11,500 rhinestones. It was modeled after a dress once worn by Marilyn Monroe.

On the other hand, Elvis Stojko is sometimes seen on the

America's Debi Thomas doing a little grunge skating.

ice wearing a hockey jersey.

Pairs skaters usually wear matching costumes. They stay away from smooth and silky fabrics. (Fingers tend to slide on them, and nobody wants to drop their partner when they're trying to do a lift.)

You'll rarely see skaters wearing much jewelry. It could get in the way and cause problems. The same is true of long hair, which also restricts a skater's vision. Women skaters with long hair usually put it in a bun, tie it with a ribbon, or hold it in place with a barrette.

MUSIC

Skating is one of the only sports performed to music. It's not just background. Music sets a mood, changes the pace of a performance, helps build drama, and keeps the crowd's interest up.

Figure skaters have performed to classical, jazz, film

scores, rock, blues, military, and disco music. Certain pieces of music seem to be chosen again and again, such as selections from *West Side Story, Fiddler on the Roof, The Nutcracker, Carmen,* or the theme from *2001: A Space Odyssey.*

Others are once-in-a-lifetime experiences. In 1993, Kurt Browning skated to a Led Zeppelin drum solo. Judges, who are usually of a different generation from the skaters, don't always look favorably upon skaters who choose very unusual music.

Most skaters, when they hear a piece of music, immediately begin thinking of it in terms of how they would skate to it. Skaters look for music that is recognizable, memorable, and loved. They also try to express a mood in their skating, so they'll select music that sounds happy, sad, funny, romantic, or whatever. You don't usually hear the words during Olympic competitions. That would distract from the skating. The music almost always comes first, and then the skater creates a dance to fit that music.

It's hard to find a four- to five-minute piece of music that has a lively beginning, slower passages in the middle, and a soaring finish. The energy level must rise and fall so the skater can time the landing of her jumps with the beat of the music. Usually it's necessary to take a longer selection and cut parts of it out to create a good piece of music to skate to.

Skaters choose their music months in advance of a competition. Then they rehearse with it hundreds of times until they know every turn, jump, and step perfectly.

At the 1990 World Professional Championships, Torvill

and Dean danced to the most outrageous music of all—one minute of total silence.

JUDGING AND SCORING

Most other sports don't need a judge to decide who is the winner. The winner of the 100-meter dash is simply the runner who crosses the finish line first. It's easy to measure which athlete pole-vaults the highest or throws the javelin the farthest. In team sports, whichever team scores the most runs, goals, touchdowns, or points wins the game.

Figure skating is different. It's a sport and an art form at the same time. It's open to interpretation which athlete put on the best performance. It's an opinion. And whenever you have opinions, you have disagreements.

When you watch figure skating on TV, sometimes you see a spectacular performance and expect the skater to receive a line of straight 6.0 marks. Instead, the marks are very low.

"Trying to figure out judging is the most frustrating exercise imaginable," according to Kurt Browning.

Figure skating is very difficult to judge. Each skater has a distinct personality. Some are spectacular jumpers. Others are more beautiful to watch. Some are very emotional and expressive. Others are more technically skilled but lack passion.

The scoring is not always fair. Skaters never want to skate first, because the first skater often receives lower marks— judges like to have room to award a spectacular performance that follows (the order is determined by a random drawing). Some judges give higher marks to skaters from their own country. Proven stars receive higher marks than young up-starts (but pros who return to amateur competition seem to be penalized).

To make certain that scoring is as fair as possible, there is a panel of nine judges, all from different countries. The judges follow strict guidelines and spot mistakes the average fan doesn't see.

The scoring system is complicated. In the simplest possible terms, the following sections describe how the judges decide which skater is the best.

SINGLES

There are two events for both men and women; a technical program and a free skate, which is sometimes called the long program.

In the technical program, each skater must execute these specific moves in any sequence:

> a double axel
> a double jump (men must do a triple jump)
> a jump combination (two jumps without a step
>   in between)
> a jump spin
> a layback spin (for men, a spin with at least
>   two changes of foot and one position
>   change)
> a spin with one change of foot and at least two
>   changes of position
> two sequences of steps or footwork done in
>   either a straight line or circular shape.

The skater receives two marks from each judge. The first mark is for technical merit—how well the required moves were executed. The second mark is for artistic impression—how well the skater used the rink; the degree of daring; the element of surprise; the height, spacing, and variety of jumps; and the overall presentation of the program.

The marks range from 0.0 to 6.0 based on this scale:

0.0—not skated

1.0—bad, very poor

2.0—poor

3.0 average

4.0—good

5.0—excellent

6.0—perfect

Many fans of skating think that the highest and lowest judge's scores are thrown out and that the rest of the scores are averaged. That's not what happens. Actually, the skater's technical and artistic mark *from each judge* are added together. Each judge's marks are converted into places related to all the skaters for that judge—first, second, third, and so on. So the skater who receives the highest mark from one judge earns a first-place vote from that judge. The skater who gets the most first-place votes from the panel of judges is the winner of the event.

Oksana Baiul and her coach, Galina Zmievskaya, reacting to Oksana's scores after the technical program in the 1994 Olympics in Norway.

In the free skate event, there are no required elements. Each skater has the freedom to create a program of jumps, spins, and interpretive moves that best displays her skills. The scoring is the same as in the technical program.

The combined placement from these two events makes up a skater's total score. If two skaters are tied at the end, the one who received the highest placement in the free skate portion is the winner. If they're *still* tied, the one with the highest artistic impression marks in the free skate portion is the winner.

Just to show how close it can be, here are the marks that Nancy Kerrigan and Oksana Baiul received in the free skate event of the 1994 Olympics:

		GBR	POL	CZE	UKR	CHN	USA	JPN	CAN	GER
Nancy	Technical	5.8	5.8	5.8	5.7	5.7	5.8	5.8	5.7	5.8
	Artistic	5.9	5.8	5.9	5.9	5.9	5.9	5.9	5.8	5.8
Oksana	Technical	5.6	5.8	5.9	5.8	5.8	5.8	5.8	5.5	5.7
	Artistic	5.8	5.9	5.9	5.9	5.8	5.8	5.8	5.9	5.9

Four judges put Kerrigan in first place, and four put Baiul in first. The judge from Germany gave both women equal totals but awarded Kerrigan a 5.8 for artistic impression and Baiul a 5.9. By that margin, Oksana won the gold and Nancy had to settle for silver.

The rules have changed over the years. It used to be that the skater with the highest *technical* marks would win in the event of a tie. So if Nancy Kerrigan had skated under the same rules that Dorothy Hamill did in 1976, *she* would have won the gold medal.

Despite all the efforts that are made to make the scoring fair, a skater is occasionally "robbed" of first place. That's what happens when human beings are judged by other human beings instead of stopwatches or measuring tapes.

PAIR SKATING

The scoring for pair skating is similar to singles, with a few minor differences.

First, the technical program has different required elements: an overhead lift, a double twist lift, side-by-side solo double jumps, a solo spin in unison, a death spiral, a spiral sequence, a step sequence, and a pair spin with at least one change of position and one change of foot.

Second, the scores for the technical program and free skate are not added together. The technical program counts for ⅓ of the total score, the free skate ⅔.

In pairs, the judges are looking for exact timing and togetherness. A couple will receive high marks when their footwork, spins, body lines, and gestures are perfectly synchronized.

ICE DANCING

Once again, the scoring is slightly different. In ice dancing there are three events: two compulsory dances (20 percent of the final score); an original dance to a specific type of music, such as tango, waltz, or rhumba (30 percent); and a free dance (50 percent). There are two sets of marks in the original dance and the free dance, and just a technical mark for the compulsory dance.

Ice dancers are judged on the flow of their program, how well they interpreted the music, originality, and difficulty. They are penalized if they separate for more than a few seconds at a time.

SCHOOL FIGURES

Until recently, the most important part of a figure skating competition was the compulsories, or "school figures."

Skaters were required to know and precisely skate 42 specific figures. Each figure consisted of two or three circles forming a variation of the figure eight. Three of these 42 figures were chosen and each skater had to trace them twice on

Jennifer Blount carefully traces a figure while a judge observes.

each foot. Both circles had to be the same size and perfectly lined up.

It was sort of like a piano player mastering scales. It took years to master the figures.

After a skater had finished a figure, the ice chips would be swept away and the judges would often get down on their hands and knees to determine which skater had executed the figure most perfectly. The scores for school figures made up 60 percent of the total score.

While the school figures *did* demonstate skill and precision, many skaters and fans felt that jumps, spins, and the free skating program were a better overall indicator of who was the best skater. And they were definitely more interesting to watch. Television viewers didn't want to watch skaters slowly carving shapes into the ice. They wanted to see spinning, leaping, and dancing.

In 1967, the International Skating Union voted to reduce the importance of school figures to 50 percent of the total score. In 1971, they decided to reduce it to 40 percent. It became 30 percent in 1975, 20 percent in 1988, and in 1990 the I.S.U. voted to eliminate school figures entirely.

Newsweek called it "the most dramatic revolution ever in the sport." It changed the nature of skating. Men and women who specialized in figures fell out of contention. Those who were terrific free skaters became superstars. TV ratings soared.

Some skating purists argued that skating was ruined, but most people agreed that the elimination of school figures revitalized skating and made it into a sport the whole world would enjoy watching.

Zeljka Cizmesija of Yugoslavia was the last skater to do a school figure in an international championship. After she completed her figures in the World Championships in Halifax, Canada, on March 7, 1990, spectators gathered around for one last look at the etchings. Some threw roses on the ice.

From that moment on, figure skating would no longer have figures.

SKATES

Compared with other sports, figure skating doesn't require much equipment. But the equipment it does require is crucial.

The blade on the skate is made from high-tempered steel

and plated with chrome or nickel. From heel to toe, there is a slight curve you can barely see, like the rockers on a rocking chair.

The blade is about ⅛ of an inch thick, and the underside is scooped out slightly to make an inside and outside edge—which are crucial to all skating moves. Whenever the skater leans to the right, the outside edge of the right skate and inside edge of the left skate are touching the ice. Without these edges, the skates would slide sideways.

The blades look as if they're attached to the exact middle of the boot, but they're not. They are placed slightly toward the inside of the sole.

Top skaters use different blades when they're skating figures (flattest, with toe picks a little higher); freestyle (shorter, more curved, deeper hollow, bigger toe picks); and ice dancing (thinnest, and shorter in the back to minimize collisions).

Blades wear down, even when they only touch ice. The best skaters will have their blades professionally sharpened after 30 or so hours of skating. Dick Button used to sharpen his skates two days before any competition.

Skate sharpening is a fine art. If the blades are *too* sharp, they bite deeply into the ice and slow down the skater. Skaters are picky and will go to the same blade specialist again and again. Some even send their skates by overnight mail to a favorite sharpener.

When you watch skating on TV, you'll notice that skaters remove their skate guards just before stepping on the ice, and put them back on as soon as they step off. They never leave their most crucial piece of equipment unprotected.

Christopher Dean watching as Gary Beacom sharpens his skates.

Skaters select their blades and boots separately, and then have them attached at a skate shop. They may pay $300 or more for the boots alone, and another $300 for blades.

At least they save money on socks. World-class skaters don't wear two pairs of thick ones, the way weekend skaters do. They want to *feel* the boot and *feel* the ice. Some even skate "barefoot."

6

❦

Superstars of the 1990s:
Profiles of Today's Greatest Skaters

Each of these great skaters is changing the sport of figure skating in some way—devising a new move, enchanting a new audience, or inspiring future generations of skaters. Perhaps one of the readers of this book will find herself or himself included in a future edition.

WOMEN

OKSANA BAIUL

Born: 1978

Hometown: Dnepropetrovsk, Ukraine

As a child: Oksana endured probably the most heart-breaking childhood of any skater. Her father, Sergei, deserted the family when she was 2. She didn't see him again until he appeared at the funeral of her mother, Marina, who died from ovarian cancer when Oksana was 13. Oksana was taken in by her coach, Galina Zmievskaya, who treated her like her own daughter. . . . As a girl, she would have to clean the ice with a shovel, because the Zamboni at her local ice rink was often broken.

Medals, honors, achievements: She won her first international competition, the 1993 World Championships (wear-

Oksana Baiul.

ing hand-me-down skates). With all the fuss over the Nancy
Kerrigan/Tonya Harding controversy, it was Oksana who
won the gold medal at the 1994 Olympics.

Did you know?: Oksana's last name is pronounced "By-
OOL." She was only the eleventh best skater in the Soviet
Union in 1991. . . . She performs six different triple jumps.
. . . She was the youngest world champion since Sonja
Henie in 1927. . . . In practice for the Olympics, she col-
lided with German skater Tanja Szewczenko and suffered a
gashed right leg and wrenched back. She had to skate with
stitches and pain killers. As she waited for her marks, she
wept uncontrollably. After Oksana was declared the winner,
coach Zmievskaya marched around wearing the medal and

boasting, "It's mine." (See also section on Viktor Petrenko.)

Off the ice: She has green eyes, and stands 5'4". . . . Her idol is ballet dancer Rudolf Nureyev (also from the former U.S.S.R.), and Oksana has pictures of him on her walls. She loves teddy bears and has a stuffed rabbit that three-time U.S. Champion Jill Trenary gave her. . . . She likes Snickers, rap music, Madonna, and Disney movies. . . . She once had a cockatoo that screamed "Hello" in Russian whenever the phone rang. . . . Her favorite book is a Russian fairy tale about a crooked horse. . . . She calls Viktor Petrenko her big brother. Today, Oksana, Victor, and Galina live and train in Connecticut.

Quote: "My mother will never leave me. We're together. She will always stay in my heart."

NICOLE BOBEK

Born: 1977

Hometown: Chicago, Illinois

As a child: Nicole's mother, Jana, is a Czechoslovakian native who fled the country in 1968. . . . Nicole never knew her father. . . . As a toddler, she would "skate" for hours to music played at home, and her mother says, "the ice was her sandbox. . . . She took her first ice-skating class at age three. Her mother would make her stand in the living room and practice spirals repeatedly. . . . Nicole and Jana have had a strained relationship over the years. . . . Nicole ran away from home at 16 and was arrested a year later for entering the home of a fellow skater. She said she was going to wait for her friend, but she had a large sum of money that had been taken from the friend's closet. She was sentenced to

Nicole Bobek.

two years probation. The charge was later dismissed.

Medals, honors, achievements: 1995 United States champion. Third in 1995 World Championships.

Did you know?: Nicole sometimes choreographs her own programs, and she is known for her graceful, swanlike spirals. . . . She became so good at making up routines on the spot that she could listen to another skater's music and create an even better routine. . . . Before she won the U.S. championship, Nicole had a reputation as a free-spirited party lover who stayed up late, showed up late, and threw tantrums. . . . She went through eight coaches in eight years before settling in with Richard Callaghan (who also coaches U.S. men's champ Todd Eldredge). Callaghan said he would coach her if she lost weight and applied herself to training.

With Callaghan's help, Nicole has become a more sophisticated, mature skater. . . . She hopes someday to become a choreographer and produce ice shows.

Off the ice: Nicole is 5'4" with blond hair and blue eyes. . . . She enjoys swimming, dancing, Rollerblading, and playing tennis. In her spare time, she likes to decorate old blue jeans with beads and rhinestones. . . . Nicole was bitten in the neck by a dog in 1994.

Quote: "Teenagers are teenagers. We go through a time when everything is pretty rough and you're not really sure what you want."

MIDORI ITO

Born: 1969

Hometown: Nagoya, Japan

As a child: The first time coach Machiko Yamada saw Midori skate, she felt there was something special. . . . Midori's parents divorced when she was 10, and she went to live with her coach, Yamada. . . . She has an older brother and a younger sister but has had little contact with her family since she left home. . . . Yamada has a daughter who is Midori's age, and the girls are like sisters. . . . Midori graduated from a women's college in Nagoya, with a degree in home economics. . . . She started taking ballet lessons when she was 11.

Medals, honors, achievements: 1989 World Champion and second in 1990, 1992 Olympic silver medalist.

Did you know?: Midori is the first World Champion from an Asian country. . . . She was seventh in the 1985 World Championships, fifth in the 1988 Olympics. . . . Midori is

Midori Ito.

one of the best jumpers in the world, including the men. She was the first female to throw a triple axel (November 2, 1988) and the first to land a triple/triple combination jump. . . . At the 1991 World Championships in Munich, Midori triple lutzed a little too close to the wall and leaped right into the stands. She came out smiling and the crowd went wild. . . . Midori is somewhat injury prone, suffering from leg and knee problems. Once she had to have surgery on her jaw. In 1985 she broke her leg in a practice session while attempting a quadruple jump before the World Championships in Tokyo. . . . There are only 28 skating rinks open year-round in all of Japan, and only 13 are competition size.

Off the ice: Midori is a huge celebrity in Japan, and

the country's most famous female athlete ever. She has done commercials for milk, cakes, and Prince Hotels; acted as a TV commentator for sumo wrestling and volleyball. . . . The Japanese press follows her the way the British press follows Princess Di. . . . Midori is only 4'7" and has slightly bowed legs. . . . She enjoys classical music—especially piano concertos—and spends hours browsing through record stores.

Quote: "All I can really do is jump. Figure skating is a matter of beauty and Westerners are so stylish, so slender. I wish I could be beautiful like them."

NANCY KERRIGAN

Born: 1969

Hometown: Woburn, Massachusetts

As a child: Nancy was afraid of the basement in her house. . . . She had a stuffed monkey named Melvin. . . . She hated green beans. . . . She has two older brothers, Mark and Michael. They used to call her "Ug," for "ugly," but in 1993 *People* magazine named her one of the 50 most beautiful people in the world. . . . Her father, a welder, worked three jobs to pay for Nancy's skating expenses. He would sometimes drive the Zamboni machine himself. . . . During high school, Nancy would go to bed at 7:00 P.M. so she could get up at 4:30 and skate. . . . She was a waitress at Friendly's after she got out of high school.

Medals, honors, achievements: 1988 National Collegiate Champion, 1992 Olympic bronze medal, 1993 U.S. Champion, 1994 Olympic silver medal.

Did you know?: Nancy likes to play ice hockey with her

brothers, and does pairs skating in exhibitions with Paul Wylie. . . . She has suffered from confidence problems and has worked with a sports psychologist on it. . . . To relax before skating, she listens to tapes of comedy teams. . . . She keeps her medals and awards in a drawer, but her two Olympic medals in a safe-deposit box.

Off the ice: Nancy has blue eyes. . . . Her middle name is Ann. . . . When Nancy was 7 months old, her mother Brenda developed multiple neuritis and lost most of her sight. She has to put her face close to a TV screen to see Nancy skate.

Nancy Kerrigan.

Nevertheless, Brenda Kerrigan is an avid skiier. . . . Nancy was engaged to be married to accountant Bill Chase in 1992, but it fell through. In 1994 she began seeing her agent Jerry Solomon and they agreed to marry in 1995. . . . She is close friends with Kristi Yamaguchi, and they were roommates during the 1992 Olympics in Albertville. Kristi calls her "Para" for "paranoid". . . . A street near the arena where she learned to skate is now called Kerrigan Way. . . . She has done endorsements with Reebok, Seiko, Ray-Ban, Disney, Northwest Airlines, and Campbell's Soup. . . . She hosted *Saturday Night Live* in 1994. In 1995 she recorded songs for a future album.

Nancy was involved in the most sensational scandal in the history of the Olympics. It took place in Detroit on January 6, 1994, at 2:30 P.M. She was coming off the ice after practice when a man ran up to her and slammed her on the right knee with a telescoping police baton. She fell to the ground and her father ran over. "It hurts, Dad!" she screamed, "I'm so scared. Why me? Why now? Why?"

The same day, tennis star Monica Seles withdrew from the first tournament she was due to compete in after her recovery from being stabbed by a "fan."

Nancy suffered a bruised kneecap and quadriceps tendon, but nothing was broken. Three weeks after the attack, she was doing triple jumps and got the go-ahead to compete in the Olympics.

The world was stunned when it turned out that the attack was masterminded by Jeff Gillooly, the husband of Nancy's teammate Tonya Harding. In the end, Gillooly spent two years in jail, and Tonya admitted she knew he was involved in the attack. She finished eighth in the Olympics, was then stripped of her 1994 U.S. Championship, fined $160,000, ordered to perform 500 hours of community service, and banned from amateur skating. Nancy came back to win the silver medal (and almost won the gold) at the Olympics.

Quote: "I was made into something I never claimed to be or wanted to be. Since I was young, I just wanted to skate. I never wanted to be famous."

MICHELLE KWAN

Born: 1980

Hometown: Torrance, California

As a child: Michelle began skating at a rink in a mall near her home. . . . When she saw Brian Boitano on TV skating in the 1988 Olympics, she decided that she wanted to jump like that. . . . When Michelle was 12, her coach, Frank Carroll, told her she needed to spend another year in the junior division. Kwan waited until Carroll had to go away for a few days, and then she applied for senior status on her own. Carroll was furious, but Michelle was accepted. . . .

Medals, honors, achievements: Finished sixth in 1993 U.S. Championships, second in 1994, and second in 1995. Fourth in 1995 World Championships.

Did you know?: Michelle was an alternate for the U.S. team at the 1994 Olympics. If Nancy Kerrigan had not recovered from the attack on her knee or Tonya Harding had been thrown off the team, Michelle would have become the youngest U.S. Olympian ever. Neither of those things happened, and Michelle graciously accepted that she did not get the chance to compete. . . . She could be the favorite at the

1998 Olympics, and she'll only be 21 when the 2002 Olympics rolls around. . . . Michelle has this fortune cookie message in her scrapbook: "YOU ARE ENTERING A TIME OF GREAT PROMISE AND OVERDUE REWARDS."

Off the ice: Michelle is 4'9". . . . She lives in Lake Arrowhead, California, with her older sister, Karen, who is also a

Michelle Kwan.

Paul Harvath

skater. Her dad works for Pacific Bell in Los Angeles, and he drives 200 miles every day to spend the nights with his daughters. Michelle's mom runs the Golden Pheasant restaurant in Torrance and joins the family on weekends. The Kwans came to America from Hong Kong in the 1970s. . . . Michelle also has an older brother named Ron.

Quote [while waiting to hear if she'd compete in the '94 Olympics]: "If somebody can't go, I'll be prepared. I think [the ruling] is fair. What I've gotten already is incredible."

KATARINA WITT

Born: 1966

Hometown: Chemnitz, East Germany

As a child: Katarina first skated when her kindergarten class visited a rink. "I made it out to the middle of the ice and I remember thinking—this is for me." . . . She has been coached by Jutta Mueller since she was 10. Jutta styled her hair, helped her pick costumes and put on makeup, and gave her 20 marks (about $7.50) when Katarina landed her first triple salchow jump.

Medals, honors, achievements: Olympic gold medalist in 1984 and 1988. Six-time European Champion, four-time World Champion (1984, 1985, 1987, 1988).

Did you know?: In the 1988 Olympics, Katarina and American Debi Thomas both skated to music from the opera *Carmen*, and "The Battle of the Carmens" was the talk of those Olympic Games. Katarina won, becoming the first woman since Sonja Henie to win back-to-back gold medals. Then she turned pro. . . . Katarina loves to flirt with the crowd while skating. She will sometimes pick a face out of the audience and perform for that person. . . . Katarina decided to come back and try for another medal in the 1994 Olympics, despite criticism that she was too old (27) and overweight, and that the younger skaters were performing jumps she could never do. Katarina kept her program secret until the Olympics, and she came out on the ice in a Robin Hood costume. She said she dressed like a man so nobody could accuse her of flirting. Her performance won over the crowd, but she finished only seventh. . . . Just before the finals, when Oksana Baiul crashed into another skater in practice, it was Katarina who picked her up off the ice. . . . In recent years, Katarina has tried to spread a message of peace through her skating, and has performed to the antiwar song "Where Have All the Flowers Gone?"

Off the ice: Katarina is 5'5" and has hazel eyes. . . . Her friends call her "Kati" and Germans call her "Katarina the Great". . . . Her mother was once a dancer and is now a physical therapist. Her father is a director at a plant and seed company. Her brother (who is coincidentally named Axel) is married to 1980 Olympic skating gold medalist Anett Potzsch. . . . Men find Katarina to be gorgeous, and at one point she filled her bathtub with 35,000 love letters. One obsessed man sent her 50 frightening letters and was arrested.

Under communism in East Germany, Katarina was followed everywhere and never allowed to be alone, and her hotel rooms were bugged. But she said she never considered defecting to the West. She had a penthouse apartment, a sports car, a country home, and other special favors few East Germans enjoyed. Once thieves broke into her apartment and stole $60,000 worth of jewelry. After communism fell in

Katarina Witt as Robin Hood.

1989, Katarina was criticized for accepting all those favors (especially after saying, "Life under communism wasn't so bad"), and even accused of being a spy for Stasi, the East German secret police.

Life under capitalism hasn't been too bad, either. She did an ice show tour with Brian Boitano, and a TV special starring the two of them won an Emmy Award. She served as a commentator for CBS at the 1992 Olympics. Katarina has made commercials for Diet Coke, earned a fortune as a professional skater, and has her own production company.

Quote: "I know this is maybe naive, but one day I hope will be peace in the world. Maybe one day the flowers will come back."

KRISTI YAMAGUCHI

Born: 1972

Hometown: Fremont, California

As a child: Kristi was born with clubbed feet. She had casts on her feet when she was just 2 weeks old, and her feet still turn in slightly. . . . She started taking ballet lessons when she was 4, and wanted to take skating lessons, but her mother said she had to wait until she could read. "I can read," Kristi announced when she came home from the first day of first grade. "Now can I go?" . . . She idolized Dorothy Hamill, and when she was 5, Kristi carried a Dorothy Hamill doll everywhere. Hamill would later visit Kristi just before the 1992 Olympic finals to wish her good luck. . . . At 8, Kristi tried to dye her hair blond so she would look like Farrah Fawcett from the TV show *Charlie's Angels*. It came out red.

Medals, honors, achievements: 1991 and 1992 World Champion. 1992 Olympic gold medalist. 1992 U.S. Champion.

Did you know?: Kristi was the first American woman since Peggy Fleming to win back-to-back World Championships, and the first American woman since Dorothy Hamill to win the Olympic gold medal. . . . She also loves pair skating, but gave up her partnership with Rudi Galino in 1990 to concentrate on singles. . . . For two years, she lived with her coach, Christy Kjarsgaard Ness, and Ness's husband, Andrew, a doctor of sports medicine who designed a weight program for Kristi. . . . She has trained at the same rink as Kurt Browning. . . . Within an 11-month stretch, she won the United States Championship, the World Championship, and the Olympic gold medal. Some year! . . . Kristi turned pro in 1992.

Off the ice: Kristi is a fourth-generation American of Japanese descent. After the invasion of Pearl Harbor, her grandfather was taken off the campus of USC and incarcerated in a camp in Colorado. . . . Kristi is 4'11". . . . She was invited to the White House and had dinner with George Bush and Boris Yeltsin. . . . She has appeared in fashion spreads for *Elle, Vogue,* and *Seventeen.* . . . She has two beauty marks, one under her left eye and one under her lips. . . . Her father is a dentist, her mother a medical secretary. Her sister, Lori, is a champion baton twirler. She also has a brother named Brett. . . . Her friends call her "Yama.". . . . She loves to shop, eat ice cream, and see movies starring Kevin Costner and William Baldwin. . . . She wears jeans and oversize sweaters, but loves jewelry. She always wears a heart earring that was given to her by skater Tai Babilonia. It's a symbol of hope and strength.

Quote: "I feel like I missed out on the regular high school social life, but that's the way I chose to be."

MEN

BRIAN BOITANO

Born: 1963
Hometown: Mountain View, California
As a child: Brian liked to pretend he was invisible. . . . None of his friends and nobody in his family skated. . . . He was inspired after seeing an Ice Follies show when he was

8. . . . He took up roller skating and would perform dangerous stunts to amaze his friends and scare the daylights out
of his parents. They thought skating lessons might save
his neck. . . . After giving him his first lesson, coach Linda
Leaver went home and told her husband that Brian would
become the world champion someday. She is the only coach
he ever had. . . . Brian wasn't interested in skating artistically
in the beginning. All he wanted to do was skate fast, jump
high, and do spins. . . . At the Ice Follies, Brian remembered
seeing a woman in an Arabian costume who was carried
around the rink on a pillow. Later, the woman, Uschi
Keszler, would become his choreographer.

Medals, honors, achievements: Four-time United States
Champion (1985-1988), 1986 World Champion. Fifth in
1984 Olympics. Won "The Battle of the Brians" against
Canadian Brian Orser to win the 1988 Olympic gold medal.

Did you know?: While his competitors skated during the

Paul Harvath

Brian Boitano.

115

1988 Olympics, Brian hid in a bathroom stall so he wouldn't have to watch. . . . He keeps his Olympic gold medal in his parents' safe-deposit box. . . . In the 1987 World Championships, he wanted to be the first to land a quadruple toe loop in competition. He fell and lost his world championship. . . . The rule that allowed professionals to return to amateur competition in 1994 was called "The Boitano Rule" because Brian argued for it. . . . He used to call himself a "technical robot" because he is such a perfectionist. . . . He invented the "Tano Triple," a triple lutz with one arm over the head. . . Singer Linda Ronstadt said her song "The Blue Train" was inspired by Boitano's skating.

Off the ice: Brian is 5'11", a giant among skaters. . . . He has hazel eyes . . . He is the youngest of four siblings. . . . His father, Lew, was a semipro baseball player. . . . Brian has had knee and back problems, and has used massage, stair-climbing machines, and acupuncture to relieve them. . . . He is the godfather of his coach's daughter. . . . He loves pasta and wants to open an Italian restaurant in San Francisco.

Quote [about his triple flip/triple toe loop combination in the 1988 Olympics]: "I went to vault off my toes and the ice just exploded under me. It felt like someone was lifting me up under the armpits and then they just set me down light as a feather."

CHRISTOPHER BOWMAN

Born: 1968

Hometown: Van Nuys, California

As a child: Christopher learned how to skate at a rink in a local mall. His mother saw him sliding around on the ice in his shoes and enrolled him in a "tiny tots" program. . . . Hockey players poked fun at him. . . . He begged his parents to get a piano. They did, but when he discovered that he couldn't play it right away, he gave it up. . . . Christopher was a child actor. He appeared in several commercials and had a small part on the TV series *Little House on the Prairie*.

Medals, honors, achievements: 1989 U.S. Champion, second in 1989 World Championships, third in 1990 World Championships.

Did you know?: Christopher is sometimes called "Bowman the Showman." He can't resist playing to the crowd, making funny faces, waving, sticking his tongue out, and winking at the camera. At exhibitions, he will sometimes climb into the stands and dance with girls. . . . At the Ice Ca-

Christopher Bowman.

Jim Graves, Icesport Press

pades, he likes to enter the rink riding a Harley-Davidson. . . .
At the 1991 U.S. Championships, he dressed all in black and
even dyed his hair black. . . . His coach, Frank Carroll, once
put Christopher into a garbage can when he misbehaved.
When Christopher left Carroll after 18 years and switched
to Toller Cranston, Bowman and Carroll stopped talking to
each other. The first thing Cranston did was have Christopher lose 15 pounds. . . . Christopher placed seventh at
the 1988 Olympics and fourth in 1992. . . . He is a spectacular triple jumper but has suffered from some back problems.

Off the ice: Christopher is 5'10". . . . Both his ears are
pierced, and he has two tattoos—a heart with devil horns on
his left wrist and a devil in diapers on his left shoulder with
the words "NOBODY'S PERFECT." . . . He is known as a
prankster, terrorizing friendly rivals like Paul Wylie and
Brian Boitano with horror movie impersonations. . . . He
calls himself "Hans Brinker from Hell." . . . His dad works for
the Los Angeles Transportation Department. . . . He was engaged to be married in 1989, but the romance dissolved
when he appeared on *The New Dating Game* and won a trip to
New Orleans. . . . He is sometimes pursued by skating
groupies.

Quote: "I don't consider myself an athlete. I'm just an average guy who doesn't like to get out of bed at 7:00 A.M. I
don't like pain. I don't like to feel cold. I enjoy the sense of
expression and achievement I get from my skating."

KURT BROWNING

Born: 1966
Hometown: Caroline, Alberta, Canada

As a child: His father, Dewey, was a cowboy who worked in rodeos, and Kurt grew up on a ranch. He had a horse named Sham when he was 4, and once helped deliver a calf. . . . Kurt started skating at 3 when his dad flooded the front yard of their house. . . . He loved playing hockey, and took up figure skating only because the hockey players weren't allowed enough ice time. . . . At Kurt's first performance, he wore a skunk costume. . . . When the rink maintenance man wasn't looking, he liked to skate right at the boards, dig in his toe pick and climb up the wall. . . . He left home at 16 to train in Edmonton

Medals, honors, achievements: World Champion in 1989, 1990, 1991, and 1993; second in 1992.

Did you know?: At the 1988 World Championships in Budapest, Kurt became the first person to land a quadruple jump in competition. He only came in sixth, but he made *The Guinness Book of World Records*. Actually, he landed his first quad in practice late one night, but just one person was watching. . . . He had automobile license plates that read "1ST QUAD."

He is probably the best skater in the world who hasn't won an Olympic medal. He finished eighth in 1988, and sixth in 1992. . . . The triple lutz jump has been his nemesis, and Kurt has been hospitalized four times because he spiked himself attempting it. He has also had back problems, and doctors warned him to quit skating or risk permanent injury. . . . Kurt claims to have invented the "waxel," a botched jump in which the skater ends up face first on the ice.

Viktor Petrenko calls Kurt "Kurtinka." Scott Hamilton calls him "Skate God." His skates cost $1,200. He likes listening to Mötley Crüe during warm-ups. If he has a good practice session, he'll go back to the same spot in the locker room the next day.

Off the ice: Kurt prefers tennis or bike riding to weight training, but he sometimes trains by running up stairs. . . . He is a bigger celebrity in Canada—where he has had TV specials, a video ("Jump"), an autobiography (*Forcing the Edge*), and commercials for Diet Coke and Toshiba—than he is in the U.S.A. He also works for the Muscular Dystrophy Association, Literacy Canada, and other charities. . . . He is close friends with Kristi Yamaguchi. . . . His father once applied for American citizenship but filled out the wrong

Paul Harvath

Kurt Browning.

forms, so Kurt was born Canadian. . . . He has an older brother and sister. . . . His hobby is leatherwork. . . . He once skied down a mountain in Switzerland with Japanese skater Midori Ito on his back. . . . When his friend Wayne Gretzky broke Gordie Howe's all time NHL points record, Kurt helped line up 1,851 pucks for Gretzky to autograph. . . . He was introduced to Queen Elizabeth in 1990.

Quote [on the first quadruple jump landed in competition]: "I went up really well. The spark that ignites to propel me high and fast enough kicked in. I was up and down—on one foot—in an instant. . . . Then I started to hear the screams. Everyone was going wild, standing up and cheering. I thought, 'Well, maybe I made it.'"

SCOTT DAVIS

Born: 1972

Hometown: Great Falls, Montana

As a child: Scott learned to skate on Gibson Pond in Montana, where there wasn't much else to do. . . . His parents divorced when he was 4. . . . He wore glasses as a boy, and they would go flying off whenever he went into a spin. So he got contact lenses. . . . When he was 9, he had his picture taken with Olympic Champion Scott Hamilton. . . . At 15, he asked his mother if he could move to Tacoma to study with coach Kathy Casey, who is also a Great Falls native. She gave him permission. Scott loved to go fast and jump, but Casey taught him how to skate for an audience. When Casey moved to Colorado Springs, so did Scott.

Medals, honors, achievements: Two-time U.S. Champion (1993, 1994).

Did you know?: A few years ago, Kathy Casey told Scott he had to take lessons in ballet and jazz dance. Scott said he didn't want to. Casey told him if he wasn't prepared to make the committment, he should pack his bags and go home to Montana. Davis took the lessons. . . . He finished eighth in the 1991 U.S. Championships, and fourth in 1992. . . . When Brian Boitano was reinstated as an amateur to compete in the 1994 Olympics, Scott figured he had no chance to make the team, so he applied to college. But then he beat Boitano to become United States Champion. His mother was so excited when he landed a triple/triple combination jump that she jumped out of her seat, smashing her camera. Scott finished a disappointing eighth in the Olympics, however.

Off the ice: Scott is 5'9", has blue eyes, and is quiet and shy. . . . His dad is a high-school football coach, his mom a nurse. . . . He has a sister named Lisa. . . . Scott enjoys water- and snow skiing, tennis, volleyball, and movies. . . . He wants someday to become a doctor of sports medicine or a physical therapist. . . . At the 1993 U.S. Championships, his pants were stolen out of his gym bag.

Quote: "My goal was to make the Olympic team in 1998, and see if I could do it in 1994. It happened."

SCOTT HAMILTON

Born: 1958

Hometown: Bowling Green, Ohio

As a child: Scott was adopted when he was 6 weeks old. . . . When he was 2, he suddenly stopped growing. Doctors were baffled. At one point, he was diagnosed with cystic fibrosis and given six months to live. His parents finally took him to Boston Children's Hospital, where it was determined he had Schwachman's Syndrome, a rare disease in which the body can't absorb nutrients from food. Scott had to have a feeding tube going into his stomach, and take food supplements intravenously. Kids made fun of his size, calling him "Peanut." . . . When he was 9, he went along to watch his sister, Susan, skate. He asked if he could try it and began skating regularly, feeding tube and all. At his physical checkup the next year, the symptoms of the disease were completely gone. . . . Scott attended three high schools his senior year due to his training.

Scott Hamilton working the crowd.

Medals, honors, achievements: Four-time World and U.S. Champion (1981–1984). 1984 Olympic gold medalist.

Did you know?: Scott carried the American flag at the 1980 Olympics (he finished fifth) and called it "one of the biggest moments of my life." . . . He got an ear infection just before the 1984 Olympics, but won anyway. He grabbed the flag and circled the ice with it. . . . Scott's mother, Dorothy, died of cancer when he was 19. Scott was going to give up skating at that time, but a wealthy couple offered to sponsor him. . . . Scott's father, Ernie, a biology teacher, suffered a slight stroke during the 1981 U.S. Championships. He hid it from Scott until Scott had won the competition. Ernie Hamilton passed away while Scott was doing TV commentary at the 1994 Olympics. . . . Scott was coached by Carlo Fassi briefly, then switched to Don Laws. . . . He doesn't like the spangles and beads other skaters wear, preferring stretch suits like those worn by speed skaters. . . . Scott loves doing backflips.

Off the ice: Scott is 5'3", 115 pounds. He freely makes fun of his size, saying he once bought a tuxedo and found a hole in the back where the ventriloquist puts his hand. . . . He lives in Colorado and is a big Denver Broncos fan. . . . For a while, Scott lived in the same Colorado apartment Dorothy Hamill once lived in. . . . He used to supplement his income by owning four video game machines at the rink where he trained. . . . Skaters Charlie Tickner and Peter and Kitty Carruthers are also adopted.

Quote: "When they introduced me as the United States Champion, it was the greatest three seconds of my life."

VIKTOR PETRENKO

Born: 1969

Hometown: Odessa, Soviet Union

As a child: Viktor began working with coach Galina Zmievskaya when he was 10 years old, and has been with her ever since. In fact, she is now his mother-in-law. In 1992 Viktor married Galina's daughter, Nina.

Medals, honors, achievements: 1988 Olympic bronze medalist. 1992 Olympic gold medalist. World Champion in 1992, second in 1991 and 1990, third in 1988.

Did you know?: Viktor does layback spins, which hardly any other male skaters can do. . . . His brother, Vladimir, is also an excellent skater, and they perform in ice shows together. . . . Viktor is a great balletic skater, and he admires Bolshoi Ballet star Vladimir Vasiliev. He also performs to rap music. . . . He was the late John Curry's favorite skater. . . . Because of the collapse of communism, Viktor has skated for three different countries in three Olympics—the Soviet Union in 1988, the Unified Team in 1992, and Ukraine in 1994. . . . The skate-sharpening machine was so poor at the Odessa Sports Palace where he used to train that Viktor bought the rink a new one. . . . He gave up the huge salary he was earning as a professional to be reinstated as an amateur and compete in the 1994 Olympics.

Off the ice: It was Viktor who asked Galina Zmievskaya to give a home to a young skater without any family—Oksana Baiul. He also paid for Oksana's skates and outfits before she became a champion herself. . . . Viktor and his wife,

Nina, moved to Las Vegas after the 1992 Olympics because a friend of his was the director of skating at Santa Fe Ice Rink ten miles away. Nina served as the director of choreography at the rink. . . . In 1994 Viktor, Nina, Galina, and Oksana moved to Simsbury, Connecticut, where a 5-million-dollar Olympic-sized skating center had been built.

Quote: "I am an athlete. The Olympics says I can come back, so I must go back."

ELVIS STOJKO

Born: 1972

Hometown: Richmond Hill, Ontario, Canada

As a child: Yes, he was named after Elvis Presley. . . . When he was just 2½ years old, Elvis saw a skater spinning on TV and decided that was what he wanted to do. His parents made him wait until he was 5 before he could start skating. . . . Kids teased him because he liked to skate, not because he had an unusual name. They probably gave Elvis's brother a harder time. His name is Attila.

Medals, honors, achievements: Finished third in 1992 World Championships, second in 1993, and became World Champion in 1994 and 1995. 1994 Olympic silver medalist.

Did you know?: He loves jumping, and is sometimes called "Air Stojko." He nearly broke his neck doing a backflip in 1993. He didn't get his legs over far enough and slammed his face into the ice. Cartilage was chipped inside his nose and a gash was opened up above his left eye. The next day, he did another backflip, this time correctly. . . . At the 1991 World Championships, he landed the first quadruple toe loop/double toe loop combination. . . . At his training rink near

Toronto there's a banner that says, "You're in Quadruple Country." . . . Elvis finished seventh at the 1992 Olympics, and upset Kurt Browning to win the 1994 Canadian Championship. He also does a wicked impersonation of Browning skating. . . . He has been criticized for lacking artistry in his skating.

Off the ice: His name is pronounced "STOY-ko," though some simply call him "The Terminator." . . . He may be just a little too far-out for the stodgy skating world. Elvis likes dirt bikes, loud music, and loud clothing. He has a black belt in karate, uses karate and kung fu moves in his skating, and sometimes skates to the music from *The Bruce Lee Story*. His parents, Steve and Irene, came to Canada from Eastern Europe in the 1950s. They own a landscaping company outside Toronto.

Quote: "Some days I get bored with training, but that's when I'm not looking for new things to do. I have to set new goals all the time, higher and higher, better and better."

PAUL WYLIE

Born: 1965

Hometown: Dallas, Texas

As a child: Paul was "dragged along" when his sisters Dawn and Clare went skating. He would play with his Tonka trucks on the ice. The management at the rink told his mother to get him on skates, and Paul liked it, to say the least. . . . He was winning tournaments by the time he was 9, though at that time he wanted to become an architect. . . . The Wylies moved to Denver when Paul was 11, and he got to see Dorothy Hamill and Robin Cousins skate there. That's

Paul Wylie.

when he got serious about skating. . . . When he was 20, Paul left home to train in Boston with Evy and Mary Scotvold, who also coached Nancy Kerrigan. Paul entered Harvard the next year.

Medals, honors, achievements: 1992 Olympic silver medalist. In the United States Championships, he finished second in 1988, 1990, and 1992, and third in 1989 and 1991.

Did you know?: Paul used to be known as a "practice skater." He couldn't handle the pressure of big competitions, probably because he is very bright and thinks too much when he should be relying on muscle memory. He finished tenth in the 1988 Olympics, tenth in the 1990 World Championships, and eleventh in 1991. He wasn't expected to do very well in the 1992 Olympics, but he went and outskated Kurt Browning, Christopher Bowman, and Todd Eldredge. After the silver medal was hung around his neck, he looked for his parents in the audience and mouthed the words, "Do you believe this?" . . . Paul turned pro after the Olympics and has become a real crowd pleaser at the Discover Cards Stars on Ice and other ice shows.

Off the ice: Paul is 5'4". His dad is a geophysicist, his mom a realtor. He is the youngest of three children. He enjoys singing a cappella. His degree from Harvard is in Government.

Quote: "No one ever took my picture before, and there were never crowds asking for autographs. There were times when I thought of giving up. But now I'm thrilled I kept at it. No matter what I wind up doing with my life, this medal will make a big difference."

PAIRS SKATING AND ICE DANCING

Couples have been ice skating together since the sixteenth century, but only in recent decades has this sport and art form become as popular as single figure skating.

What's the difference between pairs skating and ice dancing? Pairs skating is basically free skating performed in unison by partners, with the addition of overhead lifts, throw jumps, and spins. The key is perfect timing, and the movement of the two partners should be synchronized. It has been a part of the Winter Olympics since 1908, but most of the moves we see today weren't seen until the 1960s.

They were developed by a husband and wife team from the Soviet Union, Ludmila and Oleg Protopopov. The Protopopovs were World Champions from 1965 to 1968 and Olympic gold medalists in 1964 and 1968. The Russians have totally dominated pairs skating, winning an almost unbelievable nine straight Olympic gold medals since the Protopopovs started the streak. Before them, the Soviets had not won a single Olympic medal in skating.

In ice dancing, the emphasis is on rhythm, footwork, flair, and the interpretation of music. It's less gymnastic and acrobatic. Lifts above the shoulder are prohibited. So are spins that are more than one and a half revolutions. Its beauty is in creativity, choreography, and theatrics.

The first great ice dance team was Diane Towler and Bernard Ford of England, who were World Champions in 1967, 1968, and 1969. Ice dancing became a part of the Olympics in 1976. In the 1980s, it was elevated to an art form by another British couple, Jayne Torvill and Christopher Dean.

Four of today's top couples are profiled in the following section.

JAYNE TORVILL AND CHRISTOPHER DEAN

Born: 1959/1960

Hometown: Nottingham, England

How they met: Both are only children. . . . Jayne's parents ran a candy shop. Christopher's dad was an electrician. . . .

Christopher started skating because his parents lived on the outskirts of town and wanted him to meet other children. . . . He broke his leg the first week he skated. . . . They both started skating when they were 10, but didn't get together until their late teens.

Medals, honors, achievements: World Champions in 1981, 1982, 1983, 1984. Olympic gold medalists in 1984, bronze in 1994. Queen Elizabeth awarded them the "Members of the Most Excellent Order of the British Empire."

Did you know?: Before they were champions, Christo-

Torvill and Dean.

pher worked as a policeman and Jayne as a secretary. . . . They had to practice in the middle of the night, with Christopher driving the Zamboni to make the ice himself. . . . They gave up their day jobs in 1980 when the town of Nottingham gave them a grant to support their skating.

They reached their peak at the 1984 Olympics when they skated to Ravel's *Bolero*. Before that, ice dancing had been very stiff, with smiling couples performing to snippets of the most popular ballroom dances. This was the first time anyone had danced to a single, uninterrupted piece of music. It was Valentine's Day.

Bolero is the story of two lovers who are destined never to be together, so they throw themselves into a volcano. Torvill and Dean swayed for 20 seconds on their knees before they began skating. The performance ended with both of them falling down and dying on the ice. They received 6.0 marks across the board for artistic impression. Ice dancing would never be the same.

Torvill and Dean went pro after the Olympics, formed their own ice show, and had the opportunity to create innovative dances that were not allowed in amateur competition. They also performed *Bolero* over 1,000 times.

In 1994, Christopher and Jayne decided to come back and try for another Olympic medal. Dancing to Irving Berlin's "Let's Face the Music and Dance," they won the bronze. Many observers felt they were robbed of the gold.

Christopher lines up their skate guards at the side of the rink before each competition. . . . Fans throw teddy bears on the ice after each performance, and they have hundreds of them. . . . They don't just splice together tapes to make their music; they commission new music and hire 50-piece orchestras to record it.

Off the ice: Christopher and Jayne are opposites who work together perfectly. He is nervous and domineering, she relaxed and compliant. . . . Both are married to Americans. Jayne is married to Phil Christensen, a sound engineer for rock shows. Christopher married skater Isabelle Duchesnay in 1991, but they split up 18 months later. He then married Jill Trenary, the 1990 World Champion. . . . Christopher likes speed. He has raced a Porsche, flown with the Royal Air Force acrobatics team, and taken runs with the British bobsled team. . . . Both hope to open up a school for young skaters. Jayne is ready to start a family.

Quote: "We wanted to do things, skating-wise and choreographically, that hadn't been done before, to have thought behind what we're doing, so that it wasn't just coordinated movements to a piece of music. As well, it had to have rhyme and reason, a concept, a story."

—*Christopher Dean*

ISABELLE AND PAUL DUCHESNAY

Born: 1964/1962

Hometown: Montreal, Quebec, Canada, area/Lorraine region of France

How they met: Simple—they're brother and sister. . . . Isabelle and Paul grew up in the town of Aylmer, in Quebec, Canada. . . . Their father was Canadian, their mother French. As dual citizens, they could skate for either country. At first they skated for Canada, but when they were only made alternates on the Canadian team in 1985, they accepted the invitation to skate for France.

Medals, honors, achievements: Finished third in ice dancing in the 1990 World Championships, second in 1991, Champions in 1992. 1992 Olympic silver medalists.

Did you know?: As unknowns, they shocked the skating world at the 1988 Olympics when they performed "Savage Rites," a controversial number in which they danced to African drum music wearing torn animal hides. "The French pair set the rink afire," raved *Time* magazine. Christopher

The Duchesnays.

Dean of Torvill and Dean choreographed the piece. The crowd gave the Duchesnays a standing ovation, but the judges gave them eighth place (scores for artistic impression ranged all the way from 5.0 to 5.8). They toned things down for the 1992 Olympics and won the silver medal. . . . Their originality has influenced other ice dancers.

The Duchesnays have had all sorts of accidents on ice. They started out as pairs skaters but switched to dance in 1978 after Isabelle fractured her skull during training. They had to skip the 1987 French Championships after Paul skated over Isabelle's hand and slashed three of her fingers Not to be outdone, Paul had to be hospitalized with a hemorrhage in his nose after Isabelle stepped on his face. Isabelle had three knee operations in 1989. She broke a bone in her right foot in 1991, and has a screw in there holding it in place.

Off the ice: Isabelle is the team's leader, stern and dominating. Paul is shy and polite. Isabelle studied psychology in school, and Paul has a degree in molecular genetics. Isabelle was married briefly to Christopher Dean of Torvill & Dean.

Quote [about Paul]: "He's such a puppy dog off the ice, but give him a pair of skates and he turns kamikaze."

—Isabelle Duchesnay

EKATERINA GORDEEVA
AND SERGEI GRINKOV

Born: 1972/1967
Hometown: Moscow, Russia
How they met: Sergei started out as a single, but admits

Paul Harvath

Gordeeva and Grinkov.

he was terrible at it. . . . They were paired when Sergei was 15 and Ekaterina was only 10. He didn't want to skate with her, but he was *told* to by the Soviet skating authorities. . . . Ekaterina was only 14 when they won their first World Championship. She was 79 pounds, and he would pick her up and set her down like a small bird. She was a plain-looking girl, but is considered the most beautiful of all skaters today.

Medals, honors, achievements: Olympic gold medalists

for pairs in 1988 and 1994. World Champions in 1986, 1987, 1989, 1990.

Did you know?: They are sometimes called "the gorilla and the flea." Sergei is 11 inches taller, but they jump the same height, their strides match perfectly, and they spin in perfect synchrony. . . . By 1987 they were considered unbeatable. . . . They turned pro after winning their fourth World Championship. . . . When given the chance to come back and compete in the 1994 Olympics, they took it, and won the gold medal. Skating to Beethoven's *Moonlight Sonata*, they scored four 6.0s and the rest 5.9 for artistic impression. . . . In 1987, she fell on her head during training and suffered a concussion.

Off the ice: In 1991 they were still denying they were romantically involved, but they married that April. The following September their daughter, Daria, was born (in Morristown, New Jersey, of all places). . . . Ekaterina is called "Katya." . . . Her mother was a swimmer and computer specialist, her father a dancer. . . . She likes knitting, reading, and baking cakes and cookies for her teammates. . . . She understands English but is shy and doesn't speak it much. . . . She wears sneakers and blue jeans, or a long skirt when she dresses up. She puts on her own makeup, and not much of it. . . . She wants to be a coach someday. . . . Sergei's parents worked in the police department. . . . He has dimples in his cheeks. . . . He likes to play hockey. . . . They both have blue eyes. . . . They are national heroes in Russia, mobbed everywhere they go. . . . They have a home in Tampa, Florida.

Quote: "I'm so happy to skate with Sergei, who I'm so in love with. When I don't feel well, when I'm nervous, I focus on him. Our choreographer, Marina Zueva, tells me, 'Forget about everyone. Skate for Sergei.'"

—*Ekaterina Gordeeva*

ISABELLE BRASSEUR AND LLOYD EISLER

Born: 1971/1964

Hometown: Boucherville, Quebec, Canada/Seaforth, Ontario, Canada

How they met: Lloyd had three other partners before teaming up with Isabelle. When the third one dropped out because of injuries in 1986, he retired. A year later Lloyd heard that Isabelle's partner had quit, and he went to Montreal to meet her. Isabelle didn't speak any English and Lloyd didn't know much French. But when they skated, they understood each other perfectly.

Medals, honors, achievements: 1992 and 1994 Olympic bronze medalists in pairs skating. In the World Championships, they placed second in 1990, second in 1991, third in 1992, first in 1993, and second in 1994.

Did you know?: When they started to skate together, Isabelle was afraid because Lloyd is 11 inches taller than she and weighs almost twice as much. On one lift, he tosses her 12 feet off the ice, she spins three times in the air, and he catches her. . . . In the beginning, they supported themselves with a $650-a-month allowance from the Canadian government. . . . Lloyd was opposed to letting professionals return to amateur status and skate in the 1994 Olympics. He felt it held the next generation of skaters back. They are now professionals themselves. . . . They perform a hysterically funny number in which Isabelle dresses up as a man and Lloyd is dressed as a woman, doing a striptease.

Off the ice: Lloyd is into motorcycles and tattoos and likes to play hockey in his spare time. Isabelle likes to read. . . . At one time they thought about dating, but decided not to. . . . Isabelle has studied business administration. Lloyd left college to concentrate on skating. . . . They communicate in English today.

Quote: "Ten years down the road when the medals are collecting dust in a box, we'll be able to say, 'We didn't give up. We never quit.'"

—Lloyd Eisler

Paul Harvath

Brasseur and Eisler.

7

⚬⚭⚬

For Your Information . . .

YOU COULD LOOK IT UP
(BUT NOW YOU DON'T HAVE TO)

• The part of the rink where competitors go to watch their marks come up is called "the kiss and cry area," because that's what so many skaters do there.

• The 1950 World Championships were held in London, and several skaters from Communist countries used that opportunity to defect to the West. Alena Vrzanova of Czechoslovakia skipped out right after she won the Ladies World Championship. Ede Kiraly of Hungary defected after his second-place finish (to Dick Button).

Kiraly was also a great pairs skater and had won the World Pairs Championship with his partner Andrea Kekessey in 1949. When Kiraly defected, Andrea returned to Hungary. A few months later she decided to defect also, and risked her life trekking 40 miles to win her own freedom.

The last skater to defect was ice dancer Gorsha Sur, who left Russia in 1990 and came to the United States. Now he skates for the U.S. team with his American partner, Renee Roca. They were U.S. Champions in 1995 for ice dancing.

• The following ad appeared in the December 1991 issue of *Skating* magazine:

"Female dancing partner wanted for 14-year-old novice male 5'8". Acceptable height 5'2". Weight 110. Seeking serious competitor for long-term commitment. Partner experience preferred. Must be willing to relocate to New Jersey to train with Olympic dance coach. Send resume and videotape (not returnable)."

• The attack on Nancy Kerrigan in 1994 was not the first time somebody has tried to hurt the chances of another skater. In 1976, at the Olympic Village in Innsbruck, a rival's coach nearly ran Dorothy Hamill over with his car. She believes it was intentional.

And according to an anonymously written book titled *Mother's Guide to Figure Skating*, "Skaters who entertain an excellent reputation have had their laces cut, the boots covered with lipstick, screws loosened and the blades dulled with a stone or other object. Regardless of competition level it gets nauseating on occasion because of the lack of sportsmanship."

Years ago, there were even incidents in which the judges were fixed. "It was not unusual for a judge of one country to get together with a judge from another country," according to Dick Button. "The second judge would promise to support a lady competitor of the first judge's country if the first judge would support the pairs skaters of the second judge's country. The two judges might then enlist the support of a third country who had a very powerful contender for the men's title."

• Top skaters generally travel between 1,000 and 1,600 meters in a 4½-minute performance. The fastest they go is about 29 kilometers (18 miles) per hour, when they're running in for a jump. During a strenuous session, a skater's pulse rate may get up to 180 beats per minute.

• Love on the ice. Irina Rodnina and Alexsei Ulanov of the Soviet Union were in love and the greatest pairs team in the world. They won the World Championship in 1969, 1970, 1971, and 1972, plus the Olympic gold medal in 1972.

Then, Alexsei told Irina he had fallen in love with another Soviet skater, Ludmila Smirnova. Alexsei left Irina to skate with Ludmila.

But Irina Rodnina had the last word. After auditioning 100 prospective partners, she formed a new Soviet pairs team with Aleksandr Zaitsev. Together they beat Alexsei and Ludmila to win the World Championship the next six years in a row, and won the Olympic gold medal in 1976 and 1980.

Irina and Aleksandr also fell in love and got married. "They mesh like the gears in a Swiss watch," reported *Time* magazine.

Irina Rodnina is the only woman besides Sonja Henie to win three Olympic Gold medals. During her

*Irina Rodnina and her husband Aleksandr Zaitsev of the Soviet
Union (center) after winning the 1973 European Championships. In second
place (on the left) were Rodnina's previous husband, Alexsei Ulanov,
and his new wife, Ludmila Smirnova.*

remarkable career, she won ten consecutive world titles
in pairs skating.

• Divorce on the ice. Another husband-and-wife Soviet pairs team, Elena Valova and Oleg Vasiliev, won
the 1988 World Championship. They agreed to appear
at the 1992 World Professional Championships in
Maryland, but got divorced before the competition
took place. Having made the commitment, however,
the couple skated together anyway.

• Ice skaters really skate on *water*. As the blade moves
across the ice, friction makes the ice melt. As soon as
the blade passes over it, the water freezes.

• If "death spiral" sounds like a good title for a skating

book, it has been. Twice. Patricia Rosemoor used it for a Harlequin Intrigue novel about a woman who aids a victim of a rockslide. He turns out to be a famed Russian skating coach who was defecting, and they fall in love.

The other *Death Spiral* is by Meredith Phillips and is subtitled *Murder at the Winter Olympics*. A Soviet skater is killed and you have to figure out if the murderer is his girlfriend (the British ladies' champ), some political fanatics, a jealous athlete, or the KGB.

• According to the United States Figure Skating Association: "Please Note: In figure skating the term is always LADIES and not 'women.' There is a ladies' singles competition and ladies and men compete in pairs and dance."

• In St. Petersburg, Russia, one of the rinks where 1991 and 1992 World Pairs Champions Natalia Mishkutenok and Artur Dmitriev trained was closed in 1993 so it could be used to store bananas.

• Canadian Toller Cranston, who won the Olympic bronze medal in 1976, graduated with a degree in art from L'Ecole des Beaux Arts in Montreal. One of his paintings, titled *Blind Destiny*, is hanging in the World Figure Skating Museum & Hall of Fame in Colorado Springs, Colorado.

• Tai Babilonia and Randy Gardner won the 1979 World Pairs Championship for the United States. When they were first paired up as children, Tai and Randy didn't want to hold hands. Their parents had to bribe them with candy bars.

• When she was 1 year old, Natasha Kuchiki used to eat the ice off her skate blades. She grew up to win a bronze medal for the United States for pairs skating in the 1991 World Championships

• One of the rules of ice dancing is that the man must wear pants.

• At least two movies have used the plot of a figure skater and hockey player falling in love. They were *Champions: A Love Story* (1979) and *The Cutting Edge* (1992)

• Dorothy Hamill appeared on the TV show *Diff'rent Strokes*. Peggy Fleming was once on *Newhart*. Both Scott Hamilton and Debi Thomas appeared on the game show *Win, Lose, or Draw*. On one episode of *Beverly Hills 90210*, Jason Priestley did his own skating stunts.

• In the middle of the 1984 World Championships, Norbert Shramm of West Germany was in eleventh place. As he was warming up for the next part of his program, he thought the better of it and retired from skating.

• In 1967 John Baldwin won the U.S. Men's Novice Championship. Twenty years later, his son John, Jr., won the same title.

• The most recent form of ice skating is called "precision." Teams of 8 to 32 skaters perform in unison to music. The sport is hugely popular in Canada, and there are hundreds of teams in the United States, Norway,

Mexico, Japan, and many other countries. The first U.S. Precision Nationals were held in 1984. Someday precision skating may become an Olympic sport.

Precision skating was born in Ann Arbor, Michigan, in 1956, when a bunch of teenagers performed at an annual ice show. They put on a routine that resembled the Rockettes. In fact, they called themselves "the Hockettes," and the team is still going strong today.

• In 1924, two Minnesota guys named Eddie Shipstad and Oscar Johnson began performing comedy routines on skates. People seemed to like it (especially when Eddie dressed as a woman), and in 1936 they started a touring ice show called Shipstad and Johnson's Ice Follies. The show was an immediate success and toured for decades.

Comedy on ice. Eddie Shipstad and Oscar Johnson.

Comedy has become a regular feature of ice shows. Gary Beacom is known as "skating's mad artist" and will sometimes wear his skates on his hands, or do handstands on the ice while wearing a straitjacket. Even the classy Torvill and Dean perform a comedy number in which they spend the whole performance stealing hats off each other's head.

Skatable quote: "We live amid surfaces, and the true art of life is to skate well on them."

—*Ralph Waldo Emerson*

TIMELINE OF
IMPORTANT MOMENTS IN SKATING

800 B.C.: The first skates are made from animal bones.

A.D. 200: Iron skates are developed.

1500: Double-edged blades are introduced.

1683: The Edinburgh Skating Club, the first skating organization, is organized.

1772: The first textbook on skating, *Treatise on Skating*, is written by Englishman Robert Jones.

1839: Frederick Stevens starts the first skate manufacturing company in the United States.

1848: E. V. Bushnell of Philadelphia develops clamp-on skates.

1870: Toe picks are added to the front of skate blades to make new jumps and spins possible.

1874: American Jackson Haines introduces the International Style of skating in Vienna.

1881: Norway's Axel Paulsen invents the axel jump.

1892: The International Skating Union is founded.

1895: Figure skating is accepted as an Olympic sport.

1896: The first World Championships are held in St. Petersburg, Russia.

1902: Madge Syers of Great Britain enters the World Championships against men, and places second.

1903: The International Skating Union rules that men and ladies will no longer compete against each other.

1906: A separate World Championship for Ladies and Pairs is formed.

1908: Figure skating is introduced as an Olympic event in London.

1911: Ulrich Salchow of Sweden wins his tenth World Championship.

1918: Alois Lutz of Vienna creates the lutz jump.

1921: The United States Figure Skating Association is formed.

1924: The first Olympic Winter Games are held in Chamonix, France.

1936: Sonja Henie of Norway wins her third consecutive Olympic gold medal and tenth consecutive World Championship.

1948: Dick Button is the first skater to land a double axel and triple loop jumps, becoming the first American skater to win an Olympic gold medal.

1952: Ice dancing becomes a part of the World Championships.

1956: American men—Hayes Alan Jenkins, Ronald Robertson, and Hayes's brother David Jenkins—sweep the medals at the Olympics.

1961: All 18 members of the U.S. skating team are killed in an airplane crash in Brussels. The World Championships are canceled for the first time.

1962: Donald Jackson of Canada lands the first triple lutz.

1967: International competitions are skated outdoors for the last time.

1976: Ice dancing becomes an Olympic event.

1978: Vern Taylor of Canada lands the first triple axel.

1988: Kurt Browning of Canada lands the first quadruple jump.

1989: Midori Ito of Japan is the first woman to land a triple axel.

1990: School figures are eliminated from international competitions.

1991: At the World Championships, three American women sweep the medals—Kristi Yamaguchi, Tonya Harding, and Nancy Kerrigan.

1994: American skater Nancy Kerrigan is clubbed on the knee six weeks before the Olympics. Her teammate and rival Tonya Harding is implicated in the scandal, one of the most sensational in sports history.

GLOSSARY OF SKATING TERMS

Arabian: A flying spin in which the skater's body, legs, and arms are parallel to the ice. When launched on one foot and ending in a sit spin, it's called a "death drop."

Axel: The one and a half revolution "King of Jumps," and the only one that takes off from a forward position.

Camel: A spin in which one leg is extended backward, with the arms usually extended forward.

Choreography: The planning and arranging of movements, steps, and patterns in a performance.

Combination: Several jumps in succession, where the landing of one jump serves as the takeoff for the next.

Compulsory figures: A series of set patterns based on the figure eight, which had to be traced in the ice and were a big factor in skating competitions before they were eliminated in 1990. Also called "school figures."

Crossovers: The skater crosses one foot over the other to gain speed and turn corners.

Death spiral: The man swings his partner around him. She is fully extended, her head nearly touching the ice.

Edges: The two sharp sides of every skate blade on either side of the grooved center.

Flip jump: A jump that takes off with a push of the toe pick and lands with the opposite foot.

Hydrant lift: The man throws his partner over his head while skating backward, then catches her.

Lateral twist: The man throws his partner overhead in a horizontal position.

Layback: A spin in which the skater arches her back and leans her head and shoulders back.

Long program: The free skating portion of a competition, usually four minutes for ladies, four and a half for men and pairs.

Loop: A jump that takes off from the back outside edge

and lands on the same edge. In Europe, it's known as "the Rittberger," after its inventor, Werner Rittberger of Germany. A toe loop takes off from the toe pick.

Lutz: A jump that takes off from the back outside edge and lands on the back outside edge of the other foot.

Patch: A small piece of an ice rink that skaters rent to practice their figures.

Salchow: A jump that takes off from a back inside edge and lands on the back outside edge of the other foot.

Shadow skating: When two skaters perform the same movements simultaneously. "Mirror skating" is when they perform the exact *opposite* movements simultaneously.

Spiral: A long glide in which the free leg is extended up and backward.

Split: A jump in which the skater kicks her legs up and out to each side while airborne. On a Russian split, the skater touches her toes.

Spread eagle: The skater glides with her two heels facing each other and her toes facing out.

Technical program: A 2-minute-and-40-second performance set to music of the skater's choice, in which she must complete eight required elements in any sequence. Also called the "short" program.

Toe pick: The teeth on the front tip of figure skate blades. They make many jumps and spins possible.

Walley: A jump that takes off from a back inside edge and lands on the back outside edge of the same foot.

Zamboni®: The large machine that puts a new, smooth surface on the ice.

WHERE TO GO TO FIND OUT MORE

As the Toe Picks: The Skating Lover's Ultimate Trivia Challenge, by Alina Sivorinovsky (Ignel Associates, 3025 21st Ave., Suite 1010, San Francisco CA 94132, 1993)

Basic Ice Skating Skills, by Robert S. Ogilvie (Lippincott, 1968)

Dancing on Skates, by Richard Arnold (St. Martin's Press, 1985)

Dick Button on Skates, by Dick Button (Prentice-Hall, 1955)

Figure Skating with Carlo Fassi, by Carlo Fassi with Gregory Smith (Scribner's, 1980)

The Fine Art of Ice Skating, by Julia Whedon (Harry N. Abrams, 1988)

Hans Brinker, or the Silver Skates, by Mary Mapes Dodge (1865)

Ice Skating, by T. D. Richardson (B. T. Bratsford Ltd., 1956)

Ice Skating: A History, by Nigel Brown (A. S. Barnes & Company, 1959)

Ice Skating for Pleasure, by Howard Bass (Gage Publishing, 1979)

I Skate!, by Margaret Faulkner (Little Brown, 1979)

John Curry, by Keith Money (Alfred A. Knopf, 1978)

Kurt: Forcing the Edge, by Kurt Browning with Neil Stevens (HarperCollins, 1991)

Mother's Guide to Figure Skating, by T. L. Lutz (Huron Dist., P.O. Box 5584, Madison WI 53705, 1992)

Nancy Kerrigan, by Mikki Morrissette (Sports Illustrated for Kids Books, 1994)

Skaters: Profile of a Pair, by Lynn Haney and Bruce Curtis (Putnam, 1983)

Torvill & Dean, by John Hennessy (David & Charles Publishers, 1984)

A Very Young Skater, by Jill Krementz (Knopf, 1979)

Wings On My Feet, by Sonja Henie (Prentice-Hall, 1940)

Winners on the Ice, by Frank Litsky (Franklin Watts, 1979)

There is also a terrific videotape that shows many of the skaters in this book in action. It's called "Magic Memories On Ice" and was produced by CBS/Fox Video Sports. Check your local video store, or order a copy through the United States Figure Skating Association (see next page).

ICE SKATING

Write to Your Favorite Skaters

To send a letter to a famous skater, put the letter in an envelope, stamp it with first-class postage, and put the skater's name on the envelope with no address. Then fold the envelope in half, slip it inside *another* envelope, stamp that envelope and address it to:

United States Figure Skating Association
20 First Street
Colorado Springs, CO 80906

They will forward your letter to the skater. If you request an autograph or a photo from the skater, you should also include a self-addressed stamped envelope with your letter.

The Champions
Olympic, World, and United States
OLYMPIC WINTER GAMES
LADIES' SINGLES

	GOLD	SILVER	BRONZE
1908	Madge Syers	Elsa Rendschmidt	Dorothy Greenhough
London, GBR	(GBR)	(GER)	(GBR)
1920	Magda Julin-Mauroy	Svea Noren	Theresa Weld
Antwerp, BEL	(SWE)	(SWE)	(USA)
1924	Herma Plank-Szabo	Beatrix Longhran	Ethel Muckelt
Chamonix, FRA	(AUT)	(USA)	(GBR)
1928	Sonja Henie	Fritzi Burger	Beatrix Loughran
St. Moritz, SUI	(NOR)	(AUT)	(USA)
1932	Sonja Henie	Fritzi Burger	Maribel Vinson
Lake Placid, USA	(NOR)	(AUT)	(USA)
1936	Sonja Henie	Ceclilia Colledge	Vivi-Anne Hulten
Garmisch, GER	(NOR)	(GBR)	(SWE)
1940, 1944	No Olympic Games Held		
1948	Barbara Ann Scott	Eva Pawlik	Jeannette Altwegg
St. Moritz, SUI	(CAN)	(AUT)	(GBR)
1952	Jeannette Altwegg	Tenley Albright	Jacqueline du Bief
Oslo, NOR	(GBR)	(USA)	(FRA)
1956	Tenley Albright	Carol Heiss	Ingrid Wendl
Corinna, ITA	(USA)	(USA)	(AUT)
1960	Carol Heiss	Sjoukje Dijkstra	Barbara Roles
Squaw Valley, USA	(USA)	(HOL)	(USA)
1964	Sjoukje Dijkstra	Regine Heitzer	Petra Burka
Insbruck, AUT	(HOL)	(AUT)	(CAN)
1968	Peggy Fleming	Gabriele Seyfert	Hana Maskova
Grenoble, FRA	(USA)	(GDR)	(CZE)
1972	Beatrix Schuba	Karen Magnussen	Janet Lynn
Sapporo, JPN	(AUT)	(CAN)	(USA)
1976	Dorothy Hamill	Dianne de Leeuw	Christine Errath
Innsbruck, AUT	(USA)	(HOL)	(GDR)
1980	Anett Poetzsch	Linda Fratianne	Dagmar Lurz
Lake Placid, USA	(GDR)	(USA)	(FRG)
1984	Katarina Witt	Rosalynn Sumners	Kira Ivanova
Sarajevo, YUG	(GDR)	(USA)	(URS)
1988	Katarina Witt	Elizabeth Manley	Debi Thomas
Calgary, CAN	(GDR)	(CAN)	(USA)
1992	Kristi Yamaguchi	Midori Ito	Nancy Kerrigan
Albertville, FRA	(USA)	(JPN)	(USA)
1994	Oksana Baiul	Nancy Kerrigan	Chen Lu
Lillehammer, NOR	(UKR)	(USA)	(CHN)

OLYMPIC WINTER GAMES

MEN'S SINGLES

	GOLD	SILVER	BRONZE
1908 London, GBR	Ulrich Salchow (SWE)	Richard Johansson (SWE)	Per Thoren (SWE)
1920 Antwerp, BEL	Gillis Grafstom (SWE)	Andreas Krogh (NOR)	Martin Stixrud (NOR)
1924 Chamonix, FRA	Gillis Grafstom (SWE)	Willy Boeckl (AUT)	Georg Gautschi (SUI)
1928 St. Moritz, SUI	Gillis Grafstom (SUI)	Willy Boeckl (AUT)	Robert van Zeebroeck (BEL)
1932 Lake Placid, USA	Karl Schafer (AUT)	Gillis Grafstrom (SWE)	Montgomery Wilson (CAN)
1936 Garmisch, GER	Karl Schafer (AUT)	Ernst Baier (GER)	Felix Kaspar (AUT)
1940, 1944	No Olympic Games Held		
1948 St. Moritz, SUI	Richard Button (USA)	Hans Gerschwiler (SUI)	Edi Rada (AUT)
1952 Oslo, NOR	Richard Button (USA)	Helmut Seibt (AUT)	James Grogan (USA)
1956 Cortina, ITA	Hayes Jenkins (USA)	Ronald Robertson (USA)	David Jenkins (USA)
1960 Squaw Valley, USA	David Jenkins (USA)	Karol Divin (CZE)	Donald Jackson (CAN)
1964 Innsbruck, AUT	Manfred Schnelldorfer (FRG)	Alain Calmat (FRA)	Scott Allen (USA)
1968 Grenoble, FRA	Wolfgang Schwarz (AUT)	Tim Wood (USA)	Patrick Pera (FRA)
1972 Sapporo, JPN	Ondrej Nepela (CZE)	Sergei Chetverukhin (URS)	Patrick Pera (FRA)
1976 Innsbruck, AUT	John Curry (GBR)	Vladimir Kovalev (URS)	Toller Cranston (CAN)
1980 Lake Placid, USA	Robin Cousins (GBR)	Jan Hoffman (GDR)	Charles Tickner (USA)
1984 Sarajevo, YUG	Scott Hamilton (USA)	Brian Orser (CAN)	Jozef Sabovtchik (CZE)
1988 Calgary, CAN	Brian Boitano (USA)	Brian Orser (CAN)	Viktor Petrenko (URS)
1992 Albertville, FRA	Viktor Petrenko (EUN)	Paul Wylie (USA)	Peter Barna (CZE)
1994 Lillehammer, NOR	Alexei Urmanov (RUS)	Elvis Stojko (CAN)	Philippe Candeloro (FRA)

OLYMPIC WINTER GAMES
PAIRS

	GOLD	SILVER	BRONZE
1908	Anna Hubler	Phyllis Johnson	Madge Syers
London, GBR	Heinrich Burger	James Johnson	Edgar Syers
	(GER)	(GBR)	(GBR)
1920	Ludowika Jakobsson	Alexia Bryn	Phyllis Johnson
Antwerp, BEL	Walter Jakobsson	Yngvar Bryn	Basil Williams
	(FIN)	(NOR)	(GBR)
1924	Helene Englemann	Ludowika Jakobsson	Andree Brunet
Chamonix, FRA	Alfred Berger	Walter Jakobsson	Pierre Brunet
	(AUT)	(FIN)	(FRA)
1928	Andree Brunet	Lilly Scholz	Melitta Brunner
St. Moritz, SUI	Pierre Brunet	Otto Kaiser	Ludwig Wrede
	(FRA)	(AUT)	(AUT)
1932	Andree Brunet	**Beatrix Loughran**	Emilie Rotter
Lake Placid, USA	Pierre Brunet	**Sherwin Badger**	Laszlo Szollas
	(FRA)	**(USA)**	(HUN)
1936	Maxie Herber	Ilse Pausin	Emilie Rotter
Garmisch, GER	Ernst Baier	Erich Pausin	Laszlo Szollas
	(GER)	(AUT)	(HUN)
1940, 1944	**No Olympic Games Held**		
1948	Micheline Lannoy	Andrea Kekesy	Suzanne Morrow
St. Moritz, SUI	Pierre Baugniet	Ede Kiraly	Wallace Distelmeyer
	(BEL)	(HUN)	(CAN)
1952	Ria Falk	**Karol Kennedy**	Marianne Nagy
Oslo, NOR	Paul Falk	**Peter Kennedy**	Laszlo Nagy
	(FRG)	**(USA)**	(HUN)
1956	Elizabeth Schwarz	Frances Dafoe	Marianne Nagy
Cortina, ITA	Kurt Oppelt	Norris Bowden	Laszlo Nagy
	(AUT)	(CAN)	(HUN)
1960	Barbara Wagner	Marika Kilius	**Nancy Ludington**
Squaw Valley, USA	Robert Paul	Hans Baumler	**Ronald Ludington**
	(CAN)	(FRG)	**(USA)**
1964	Ludmila Belousova	Marika Kilius	Debbi Wilkes
Innsbruck, AUT	Oleg Protopopov	Hans Baumler*	Guy Revell
	(URS)	(FRG)	(CAN)

* Proven after the games that they had signed a show contract prior to the games. Silver went to Revell and Wilkes. Bronze went to Ronald and Vivian Joseph, USA.

1968	Ludmila Protopopov	Tatiana Joukchesternava	Margot Glockshuber
Grenoble, FRA	Oleg Protopopov	Alexandr Gorelik	Wolfgang Danne
	(URS)	(URS)	(FRG)
1972	Irina Rodnina	Ludmila Smirnova	Manuela Gross
Sapporo, JPN	Alexei Ulanov	Andrei Suraikin	Uwe Kagelmann
	(URS)	(URS)	(GDR)
1976	Irina Rodnina	Romy Kermer	Manuela Gross
Innsbruck, AUT	Aleksandr Zaitsev	Rolf Osterreich	Uwe Kagelmann
	(URS)	(GDR)	(GDR)
1980	Irina Rodnina	Marina Cherkosova	Manuella Mager
Lake Placid, USA	Aleksandr Zaitsev	Sergei Shakrai	Uwe Bewersdorff
	(URS)	(URS)	(GDR)
1984	Elena Valova	**Caitlin Carruthers**	Larissa Selezneva
Sarajevo, YUG	Oleg Vassiliev	**Peter Carruthers**	Oleg Makarov
	(URS)	**(USA)**	(URS)

ICE SKATING

	GOLD	SILVER	BRONZE
1988 Calgary, CAN	Ekaterina Gordeeva Sergei Grinkov (URS)	Elena Valova Oleg Vasiliev (URS)	Jill Watson Peter Oppegard (USA)
1992 Albertville, FRA	Natalia Mishkutenok Artur Dmitriev (EUN)	Elena Bechke Denis Petrov (EUN)	Isabelle Brasseur Lloyd Eisler (CAN)
1994 Lillehammer, NOR	Ekaterina Gordeeva Sergei Grinkov (RUS)	Natalia Mishkutenok Artur Dmitriev (RUS)	Isabelle Brasseur Lloyd Eisler (CAN)

OLYMPIC WINTER GAMES
ICE DANCING

	GOLD	SILVER	BRONZE
1976	Ludmila Pakhomova	Irina Moiseeva	Colleen O'Connor
Innsbruck, AUT	Aleksandr Gorshkov	Andrei Minenkov	Jim Millns
	(URS)	(URS)	(USA)
1980	Gennadi Karponosov	Krisztina Regoczy	Irina Moiseeva
Lake Placid, USA	Natalia Lininchuk	Andras Sallay	Andrei Minenkov
	(URS)	(HUN)	(URS)
1984	Jayne Torvill	Natalias Bestemianova	Marina Klimova
Sarajevo, YUG	Christopher Dean	Andrei Bukin	Sergei Ponomarenko
	(GBR)	(URS)	(URS)
1988	Natalia Bestemianova	Marina Klimova	Tracy Wilson
Calgary, CAN	Andrei Bukin	Sergei Ponomarenko	Robert McCall
	(URS)	(URS)	(CAN)
1992	Marina Klimova	Isabelle Duchesnay	Maia Usova
Albertville, FRA	Sergei Ponomarenko	Paul Duchesnay	Alexander Zhulin
	(EUN)	(FRA)	(EUN)
1994	Oksana Gritchuk	Maia Usova	Jayne Torvill
Lillehammer, NOR	Evgeni Platov	Alexander Zhulin	Christopher Dean
	(EUN)	(RUS)	(GBR)

WORLD CHAMPIONSHIPS
LADIES' SINGLES

1906	Madge Syers (GBR)	1925	Herma Jaross-Szabo (AUT)	1938	Megan Taylor (GBR)
1907	Madge Syers (GBR)	1926	Herma Jaross-Szabo (AUT)	1939	Megan Taylor (GBR)
1908	Lily Kronberger (HUN)	1927	Sonja Henie (NOR)	1940–1946	No Championship Held
1909	Lily Kronberger (HUN)	1928	Sonja Henie (NOR)	1947	Barbara Ann Scott (CAN)
1910	Lily Kronberger (HUN)	1929	Sonja Henie (NOR)	1948	Barbara Ann Scott (CAN)
1911	Lily Kronberger (HUN)	1930	Sonja Henie (NOR)	1949	Alena Vrzanova (CZE)
1912	Opika von Horvath (HUN)	1931	Sonja Henie (NOR)	1950	Alena Vrzanova (CZE)
1913	Opika von Horvath (HUN)	1932	Sonja Henie (NOR)	1951	Jeannette Altwegg (GBR)
1914	Opika von Horvath (HUN)	1933	Sonja Henie (NOR)	1952	Jacqueline du Bief (FRA)
1915–1921	No Championship Held	1934	Sonja Henie (NOR)	1953	Tenley Albright (USA)
1922	Herma Plank-Szabo (AUT)	1935	Sonja Henie (NOR)	1954	Gundi Busch (FRG)
1923	Herma Plank-Szabo (AUT)	1936	Sonja Henie (NOR)	1955	Tenley Albright (USA)
1924	Herma Plank-Szabo (AUT)	1937	Cecilia Colledge (GBR)	1956	Carol Heiss (USA)

159

WORLD CHAMPIONSHIPS

LADIES' SINGLES

1957	**Carol Heiss** (USA)	1970	Gabriele Seyfert (GDR)	1983	**Rosalynn Sumners** (USA)
1958	**Carol Heiss** (USA)	1971	Beatrix Schuba (AUT)	1984	Katarina Witt (GDR)
1958	**Carol Heiss** (USA)	1972	Beatrix Schuba (AUT)	1985	Katarina Witt (GDR)
1960	**Carol Heiss** (USA)	1973	Karen Magnussen (CAN)	1986	**Debi Thomas** (USA)
1961	**No Championship Held**	1974	Christine Errath (GDR)	1987	Katarina Witt (GDR)
1962	Sjouke Dijkstra (HOL)	1975	Dianne de Leeuw (HOL)	1988	Katarina Witt (GDR)
1963	Sjouke Dijkstra (HOL)	1976	**Dorothy Hamill** (USA)	1989	Midori Ito (JPN)
1964	Sjouke Dijkstra (HOL)	1977	**Linda Fratianne** (USA)	1990	**Jill Trenary** (USA)
1965	Petra Burka (CAN)	1978	Anett Poetzch (GDR)	1991	**Kristi Yamaguchi** (USA)
1966	**Peggy Flemming** (USA)	1979	**Linda Fratianne** (USA)	1992	**Kristi Yamaguchi** (USA)
1967	**Peggy Flemming** (USA)	1980	Anett Poetzch (GDR)	1993	Oksana Baiul (UKR)
1968	**Peggy Flemming** (USA)	1981	Denise Biellmann (SUI)	1994	Yuka Sato (JPN)
1969	Gabriele Seyfert (GDR)	1982	**Elaine Zayak** (USA)	1995	Chen Lu (CHN)

WORLD CHAMPIONSHIPS
MENS' SINGLES

1896	Gilbert Fuchs (GER)	1931	Karl Schafer (AUT)	1967	Emmerich Danzer (AUT)
1897	Gustav Hugel (AUT)	1932	Karl Schafer (AUT)	1968	Emmerich Danzer (AUT)
1898	Henning Grenander (SWE)	1933	Karl Schafer (AUT)	1969	**Tim Wood (USA)**
1899	Gustav Hugel (AUT)	1934	Karl Schafer (AUT)	1970	**Tim Wood (USA)**
1900	Gustav Hugel (AUT)	1935	Karl Schafer (AUT)	1971	Ondrej Nepela (CZE)
1901	Ulrich Salchow (SWE)	1936	Karl Schafer (AUT)	1972	Ondrej Nepela (CZE)
1901	Ulrich Salchow (SWE)	1937	Felix Kaspar (AUT)	1973	Ondrej Nepela (CZE)
1902	Ulrich Salchow (SWE)	1938	Felix Kaspar (AUT)	1974	Jan Hoffmann (GDR)
1903	Ulrich Salchow (SWE)	1939	Graham Sharp (GBR)	1975	Sergei Volkov (URS)
1904	Ulrich Salchow (SWE)	1940-1946	**No Championship Held**	1976	John Curry (GBR)
1905	Ulrich Salchow (SWE)	1947	Hans Gerschwiler (SUI)	1977	Vladimir Kovalev (URS)
1906	Gilbert Fuchs (GER)	1948	**Richard Button (USA)**	1978	**Charles Tickner (USA)**
1907	Ulrich Salchow (SWE)	1949	**Richard Button (USA)**	1979	Vladimir Kovalev (URS)
1908	Ulrich Salchow (SWE)	1950	**Richard Button (USA)**	1980	Jan Hoffmann (GDR)
1909	Ulrich Salchow (SWE)	1951	**Richard Button (USA)**	1981	**Scott Hamilton (USA)**
1910	Ulrich Salchow (SWE)	1952	**Richard Button (USA)**	1982	**Scott Hamilton (USA)**
1911	Ulrich Salchow (SWE)	1953	Hayes Jenkins (USA)	1983	**Scott Hamilton (USA)**
1912	Fritz Kachler (AUT)	1954	Hayes Jenkins (USA)	1984	**Scott Hamilton (USA)**
1913	Fritz Kachler (AUT)	1955	Hayes Jenkins (USA)	1985	Alexandr Fadeev (URS)
1914	Gosta Sandahl (SWE)	1956	Hayes Jenkins (USA)	1986	**Brian Boitano (USA)**
1915-1921	**No Championship Held**	1957	**David Jenkins (USA)**	1987	Brian Orser (CAN)
1922	Gillis Grafstrom (SWE)	1958	**David Jenkins (USA)**	1988	**Brian Boitano (USA)**
1923	Fritz Kachler (AUT)	1959	**David Jenkins (USA)**	1989	Kurt Browning (CAN)
1924	Gillis Grafstrom (SWE)	1960	Alain Giletti (FRA)	1990	Kurt Browning (CAN)
1925	Willy Boeckl (AUT)	1961	**No Championship Held**	1991	Kurt Browning (CAN)
1926	Willy Boeckl (AUT)	1962	Donald Jackson (CAN)	1992	Viktor Petrenko (CIS)
1927	Willy Boeckl (AUT)	1963	Donald McPherson (CAN)	1993	Kurt Browning (CAN)
1928	Willy Boeckl (AUT)	1964	Manfred Schnelldorfer (CAN)	1994	Elvis Stojko (CAN)
1929	Gillis Grafstrom (SWE)	1965	Alain Calmat (FRA)	1995	Elvis Stojko (CAN)
1930	Karl Schafer (AUT)	1966	Emmerich Danzer (AUT)		

WORLD CHAMPIONSHIPS
PAIRS

1908	Anna Hubler Heinrich Burger (GER)	1932	Andree Brunet Pierre Brunet (FRA)	1956	Elisabeth Schwarz Kurt Oppelt (AUT)
1909	Phyllis Johnson James Johnson (GBR)	1933	Emilie Rotter Laszlo Szollas (HUN)	1957	Barbara Wagner Robert Paul (CAN)
1910	Anna Hubler Heinrich Burger (GER)	1934	Emilie Rotter Laszlo Szollas (HUN)	1958	Barbara Wagner Robert Paul (CAN)
1911	Ludowika Eilers Walter Jakobsson (FIN)	1935	Emilie Rotter Laszlo Szollas (HUN)	1959	Barbara Wagner Robert Paul (CAN)
1912	Phyllis Johnson James Johnson (GBR)	1936	Maxi Herber Ernst Baier (GER)	1960	Barbara Wagner Robert Paul (CAN)
1913	Helene Engelmann Karl Mejstrik (AUT)	1937	Maxi Herber Ernst Baier (GER)	1961	No Championship Held
1914	Ludowika Jakobsson Walter Jakobsson (FIN)	1938	Maxi Herber Ernst Baier (GER)	1962	Maria Jelinek Otto Jelinek (CAN)
1915–1921	No Championship Held	1939	Maxi Herber Ernst Baier (GER)	1963	Marika Kilius Hans Baumler (FRG)
1922	Helene Engelmann Alfred Berger (AUT)	1940–1946	No Championship Held	1964	Marika Kilius Hans Baumler (FRG)
1923	Ludowika Jakobsson Walter Jakobsson (FIN)	1947	Micheline Lannoy Pierre Baugniet (BEL)	1965	Ludmila Belousova Oleg Protopopov (URS)
1924	Helene Engelmann Alfred Berger (AUT)	1948	Micheline Lannoy Pierre Baugniet (BEL)	1966	Ludmila Belousova Oleg Protopopov (URS)
1925	Herma Jaross-Szabo Ludwig Wrede (AUT)	1949	Andrea Kekesy Ede Kiraly (HUN)	1967	Ludmila Belousova Oleg Protopopov (URS)
1926	Andree Brunet Pierre Brunet (FRA)	1950	Karol Kennedy Peter Kennedy (USA)	1968	Ludmila Belousova Oleg Protopopov (URS)
1927	Herma Jaross-Szabo Ludwig Wrede (AUT)	1951	Ria Falk Paul Falk (FRG)	1969	Irina Rodnina Alexsei Ulanov (URS)
1928	Andree Brunet Pierre Brunet (FRA)	1952	Ria Falk Paul Falk (FRG)	1970	Irina Rodnina Alexsei Ulanov (URS)
1929	Lilly Scholz Otto Kaiser (AUT)	1953	Jennifer Nicks John Nicks (GBR)	1971	Irina Rodnina Alexsei Ulanov (URS)
1930	Andree Brunet Pierre Brunet (FRA)	1954	Frances Dafoe Norris Bowden (CAN)	1972	Irina Rodnina Alexsei Ulanov (URS)
1931	Emilie Rotter Laszlo Szollas (HUN)	1955	Frances Dafoe Norris Bowden (CAN)	1973	Irina Rodnina Alexandr Zaitsev (URS)

WORLD CHAMPIONSHIPS

PAIRS

1974	Irina Rodnina Alexandr Zaitsev (URS)	1982	Sabine Baess Tassilo Thierbach (GDR)	1990	Ekaterina Gordeeva Sergei Grinkov (URS)
1975	Irina Rodnina Alexandr Zaitsev (URS)	1983	Elena Valova Oleg Vasiliev (URS)	1991	Natalia Mishkutenok Artur Dmitriev (URS)
1976	Irina Rodnina Alexandr Zaitsev (URS)	1984	Barbara Underhill Paul Martini (CAN)	1992	Natalia Mishkutenok Artur Dmitriev (CIS)
1977	Irina Rodnina Alexandr Zaitsev (URS)	1985	Elena Valova Oleg Vasiliev (URS)	1993	Isabelle Brasseur Lloyd Eisler (CAN)
1978	Irina Rodnina Alexandr Zaitsev (URS)	1986	Ekaterina Gordeeva Sergei Grinkov (URS)	1994	Eugenia Shishkova Vadim Naumov (RUS)
1979	Tai Babilonia Randy Gardner (USA)	1987	Ekaterina Gordeeva Sergei Grinkov (URS)	1995	Radka Kovarikova Rene Novotny (CZK)
1980	Marina Cherkasova Sergei Shakhrai (URS)	1988	Elena Valova Oleg Vasiliev (URS)		
1981	Irina Vorobieva Igor Lisovsky (URS)	1989	Ekaterina Gordeeva Sergei Grinkov (URS)		

WORLD CHAMPIONSHIPS
ICE DANCING

1952	Jean Westwood Lawrence Demmy (GBR)	1967	Diane Towler Bernard Ford (GBR)	1982	Jayne Torvill Christopher Dean (GBR)
1953	Jean Westwood Lawrence Demmy (GBR)	1968	Diane Towler Bernard Ford (GBR)	1983	Jayne Torvill Christopher Dean (GBR)
1954	Jean Westwood Lawrence Demmy (GBR)	1969	Diane Towler Bernard Ford (GBR)	1984	Jayne Torvill Christopher Dean (GBR)
1955	Jean Westwood Lawrence Demmy (GBR)	1970	Ludmila Pakhomova Aleksandr Gorshkov (URS)	1985	Natalia Bestemianova Andrei Bukin (URS)
1956	Pamela Weight Paul Thomas (GBR)	1971	Ludmila Pakhomova Aleksandr Gorshkov (URS)	1986	Natalia Bestemianova Andrei Bukin (URS)
1957	June Markham Courtney Jones (GBR)	1972	Ludmila Pakhomova Aleksandr Gorschkov (URS)	1987	Natalia Bestemianova Andrei Bukin (URS)
1958	June Markham Courtney Jones (GBR)	1973	Ludmila Pakhomova Aleksandr Gorshkov (URS)	1988	Natalia Bestemianova Andrei Bukin (URS)
1959	Doreen Denny Courtney Jones (GBR)	1974	Ludmila Pakhomova Aleksandr Gorshkov (URS)	1989	Marina Klimova Sergei Ponomarenko (URS)
1960	Doreen Denny Courtney Jones (GBR)	1975	Irina Moiseeva Andrei Minenkov (URS)	1990	Marina Klimova Sergei Ponomarenko (URS)
1961	No Competition Held	1976	Ludmila Pakhomova Aleksandr Gorshkov (URS)	1991	Isabelle Duchesnay Paul Duchesnay (FRA)
1962	Eva Romanova Pavel Roman (CZE)	1977	Irina Moiseeva Andrei Minenkov (URS)	1992	Marina Klimova Sergei Ponomarenko (CIS)
1963	Eva Romanova Pavel Roman (CZE)	1978	Natalia Linichuk Gennadi Karponosov (URS)	1993	Maia Usova Alexandr Zhulin (RUS)
1964	Eva Romanova Pavel Roman (CZE)	1979	Natalia Linichuk Gennadi Karponosov (URS)	1994	Oksana Gritchuk Evgeni Platov (RUS)
1965	Eva Romanova Pavel Roman (CZE)	1980	Krisztina Regoeczy Andras Sallay (HUN)	1995	Oksana Gritchuk Evgeni Platov (RUS)
1966	Diane Towler Bernard Ford (GBR)	1981	Jayne Torvill Christopher Dean (GBR)		

UNITED STATES
FIGURE SKATING CHAMPIONSHIPS

LADIES' SINGLES

1914	Theresa Weld	1956	Tenley Albright
1915–1917	**No Competition Held**	1957	Carol Heiss
1918	Rosemary Beresford	1958	Carol Heiss
1919	**No Competition Held**	1959	Carol Heiss
1920	Theresa Weld	1960	Carol Heiss
1921	Theresa Blanchard	1961	Laurence Owen
1922	Theresa Blanchard	1962	Barbara Roles
1923	Theresa Blanchard	1963	Lorraine Hanlon
1924	Theresa Blanchard	1964	Peggy Fleming
1925	Beatrix Loughran	1965	Peggy Fleming
1926	Beatrix Loughran	1966	Peggy Fleming
1927	Beatrix Loughran	1967	Peggy Fleming
1928	Maribel Vinson	1968	Peggy Fleming
1929	Maribel Vinson	1969	Janet Lynn
1930	Maribel Vinson	1970	Janet Lynn
1931	Maribel Vinson	1971	Janet Lynn
1932	Maribel Vinson	1972	Janet Lynn
1933	Maribel Vinson	1973	Janet Lynn
1934	Suzanne Davis	1974	Dorothy Hamill
1935	Maribel Vinson	1975	Dorothy Hamill
1936	Maribel Vinson	1976	Dorothy Hamill
1937	Maribel Vinson	1977	Linda Fratianne
1938	Joan Tozzer	1978	Linda Fratianne
1939	Joan Tozzer	1979	Linda Fratianne
1940	Joan Tozzer	1980	Linda Fratianne
1941	Jane Vaughn	1981	Elaine Zayak
1942	Jane Vaughn	1982	Rosalynn Sumners
1943	Gretchen Merrill	1983	Rosalynn Sumners
1944	Gretchen Merrill	1984	Rosalynn Sumners
1945	Gretchen Merrill	1985	Tiffany Chin
1946	Gretchen Merrill	1986	Debi Thomas
1947	Gretchen Merrill	1987	Jill Trenary
1948	Gretchen Merrill	1988	Debi Thomas
1949	Yvonne C. Sherman	1989	Jill Trenary
1950	Yvonne C. Sherman	1990	Jill Trenary
1951	Sonya Klopfer	1991	Tonya Harding
1952	Tenley Albright	1992	Kristi Yamaguchi
1953	Tenley Albright	1993	Nancy Kerrigan
1954	Tenley Albright	1994	Vacant*
1955	Tenley Albright	1995	Nicole Bobek

*Tonya Harding won the U.S. Championship but was stripped of her title.

UNITED STATES
FIGURE SKATING CHAMPIONSHIPS

MENS' SINGLES

1914	Norman M. Scott	1957	David Jenkins
1915–1917	**No Competition Held**	1958	David Jenkins
1918	Nathaniel Niles	1959	David Jenkins
1919	**No Competition Held**	1960	David Jenkins
1920	Sherwin Badger	1961	Bradley Lord
1921	Sherwin Badger	1962	Monty Hoyt
1922	Sherwin Badger	1963	Thomas Litz
1923	Sherwin Badger	1964	Scott Allen
1924	Sherwin Badger	1965	Gary Visconti
1925	Nathaniel Niles	1966	Scott Allen
1926	Chris Christenson	1967	Gary Visconti
1927	Nathaniel Niles	1968	Tim Wood
1928	Roger Turner	1969	Tim Wood
1929	Roger Turner	1970	Tim Wood
1930	Roger Turner	1971	J. Misha Petkevich
1931	Roger Turner	1972	Kenneth Shelley
1932	Roger Turner	1973	Gordon McKellen
1933	Roger Turner	1974	Gordon McKellen
1934	Roger Turner	1975	Gordon McKellen
1935	Robin Lee	1976	Terry Kubicka
1936	Robin Lee	1977	Charles Tickner
1937	Robin Lee	1978	Charles Tickner
1938	Robin Lee	1979	Charles Tickner
1939	Robin Lee	1980	Charles Tickner
1940	Eugene Turner	1981	Scott Hamilton
1941	Eugene Turner	1982	Scott Hamilton
1942	Bobby Specht	1983	Scott Hamilton
1943	Arthur Vaughn	1984	Scott Hamilton
1944–1945	**No Competition Held**	1985	Brian Boitano
1946	Richard Button	1986	Brian Boitano
1947	Richard Button	1987	Brian Boitano
1948	Richard Button	1988	Brian Boitano
1949	Richard Button	1989	Christopher Bowman
1950	Richard Button	1990	Todd Eldredge
1951	Richard Button	1991	Todd Eldredge
1952	Richard Button	1992	Christopher Bowman
1953	Hayes A. Jenkins	1993	Scott Davis
1954	Hayes A. Jenkins	1994	Scott Davis
1955	Hayes A. Jenkins	1995	Todd Eldredge
1956	Hayes A. Jenkins		

UNITED STATES
FIGURE SKATING CHAMPIONSHIPS
PAIRS

Year	Champions	Year	Champions	Year	Champions
1914	Jeanne Chevalier / Norman M. Scott	1943	Doris Schubach / Walter Noffke	1970	Jojo Starbuck / Kenneth Shelley
1915–1917	No Competition Held	1944	Doris Schubach / Walter Noffke	1971	Jojo Starbuck / Kenneth Shelley
1918	Theresa Weld / Nathaniel Niles	1945	Donna J. Pospisil / Jean P. Brunet	1972	Jojo Starbuck / Kenneth Shelley
1919	No Competition Held	1946	Donna J. Pospisil / Jean P. Brunet	1973	Melissa Militano / Mark Militano
1920	Theresa Weld / Nathaniel Niles	1947	Yvonne Sherman / Robert Swenning	1974	Melissa Militano / Johnny Johns
1921	Theresa Blanchard / Nathaniel Niles	1948	Karol Kennedy / Peter Kennedy	1975	Melissa Militano / Johnny Johns
1922	Theresa Blanchard / Nathaniel Niles	1949	Karol Kennedy / Peter Kennedy	1976	Tai Babilonia / Randy Gardner
1923	Theresa Blanchard / Nathaniel Niles	1950	Karol Kennedy / Peter Kennedy	1977	Tai Babilonia / Randy Gardner
1924	Theresa Blanchard / Nathaniel Niles	1951	Karol Kennedy / Peter Kennedy	1978	Tai Babilonia / Randy Gardner
1925	Theresa Blanchard / Nathaniel Niles	1952	Karol Kennedy / Peter Kennedy	1979	Tai Babilonia / Randy Gardner
1926	Theresa Blanchard / Nathaniel Niles	1953	Carole Ormaca / Robin Greiner	1980	Tai Babilonia / Randy Gardner
1927	Theresa Blanchard / Nathaniel Niles	1954	Carole Ormaca / Robin Greiner	1981	Caitlin Carruthers / Peter Carruthers
1928	Maribel Vinson / Thornton Coolidge	1955	Carole Ormaca / Robin Greiner	1982	Caitlin Carruthers / Peter Carruthers
1929	Maribel Vinson / Thornton Coolidge	1956	Carole Ormaca / Robin Greiner	1983	Caitlin Carruthers / Peter Carruthers
1930	Beatrix Loughran / Sherwin Badger	1957	Nancy Rouillard / Ronald Ludington	1984	Caitlin Carruthers / Peter Carruthers
1931	Beatrix Loughran / Sherwin Badger	1958	Nancy Ludington / Ronald Ludington	1985	Jill Watson / Peter Oppegard
1932	Beatrix Loughran / Sherwin Badger	1959	Nancy Ludington / Ronald Ludington	1986	Gillian Wachsman / Todd Waggoner
1933	Maribel Vinson / George Hill	1960	Nancy Ludington / Ronald Ludington	1987	Jill Watson / Peter Oppegard
1934	Grace Madden / J. Lester Madden	1961	Maribel Owen / Dudley Richards	1988	Jill Watson / Peter Oppegard
1935	Maribel Vinson / George Hill	1962	Dorothyann Nelson / Pieter Kollen	1989	Kristi Yamaguchi / Rudi Galindo
1936	Maribel Vinson / George Hill	1963	Judianne Fotheringill / Jerry Fotheringill	1990	Kristi Yamaguchi / Rudi Galindo
1937	Maribel Vinson / George Hill	1964	Judianne Fotheringill / Jerry Fotheringill	1991	Natasha Kuchiki / Todd Sand
1938	Joan Tozzer / Bernard Fox	1965	Vivian Joseph / Ronald Joseph	1992	Calla Urbanski / Rocky Marval
1939	Joan Tozzer / Bernard Fox	1966	Cynthia Kauffman / Ronald Kauffman	1993	Calla Urbanski / Rocky Marval
1940	Joan Tozzer / Bernard Fox	1967	Cynthia Kauffman / Ronald Kauffman	1994	Jenni Meno / Todd Sand
1941	Donna Atwood / Eugene Turner	1968	Cynthia Kauffman / Ronald Kauffman	1995	Jenni Meno / Todd Sand
1942	Doris Schubach / Walter Noffke	1969	Cynthia Kauffman / Ronald Kauffman		

UNITED STATES
FIGURE SKATING CHAMPIONSHIPS

ICE DANCING

1936	Marjorie Parker Joseph Savage	1956	Joan Zamboni Roland Junso	1976	Colleen O'Connor Jim Millns
1937	Nettie Prantell Harold Hartshorne	1957	Sharon McKenzie Bert Wright	1977	Judy Genovesi Kent Weigle
1938	Nettie Prantel Harold Hartshorne	1958	Andree Anderson Donald Jacoby	1978	Stacey Smith John Summers
1939	Sandy MacDonald Harold Hartshorne	1959	Andree Jacoby Donald Jacoby	1979	Stacey Smith John Summers
1940	Sandy MacDonald Harold Hartshorne	1960	Margie Ackles Charles Phillips	1980	Stacey Smith John Summers
1941	Sandy MacDonald Harold Hartshorne	1961	Dianne Sherbloom Larry Pierce	1981	Judy Blumberg Michael Seibert
1942	Edith Whetstone Alfred Richards	1962	Yvonne Littlefield Peter Betts	1982	Judy Blumberg Michael Seibert
1943	Marcella May James Lochead	1963	Sally Schantz Stanley Urban	1983	Judy Blumberg Michael Seibert
1944	Marcella May James Lochead	1964	Darlene Streich Charles Fetter	1984	Judy Blumberg Michael Seibert
1945	Kathe Williams Robert Swenning	1965	Kristin Fortune Dennis Sveum	1985	Judy Blumberg Michael Seibert
1946	Anne Davies Carleton Hoffner	1966	Kristin Fortune Dennis Sveum	1986	Renee Roca Donald Adair
1947	Lois Waring Walter Bainbridge	1967	Lorna Dyer John Carrell	1987	Suzanne Semanick Scott Gregory
1948	Lois Waring Walter Bainbridge	1968	Judy Schwomeyer James Sladky	1988	Suzanne Semanick Scott Gregory
1949	Lois Waring Walter Bainbridge	1969	Judy Schwomeyer James Sladky	1989	Susan Wynne Joseph Druar
1950	Lois Waring Michael McGean	1970	Judy Schwomeyer James Sladky	1990	Susan Wynne Joseph Druar
1951	Carmel Bodel Edward Bodel	1971	Judy Schwomeyer James Sladky	1991	Elizabeth Punsalan Jerod Swallow
1952	Lois Waring Michael McGean	1972	Judy Schwomeyer James Sladky	1992	April Sargent Russ Witherby
1953	Carol Ann Peters Daniel Ryan	1973	Mary Campbell Johnny Johns	1993	Renee Roca Gorsha Sur
1954	Carmel Bodel Edward Bodel	1974	Colleen O'Connor Jim Millns	1994	Elizabeth Punsalan Jerod Swallow
1955	Carmel Bodel Edward Bodel	1975	Colleen O'Connor Jim Millns	1995	Renee Roca Gorsha Sur

About the Author

Dan Gutman is the co-author of *Taking Flight: My Story by Vicki Van Meter* (Viking). He is best known for his many books about the National Pastime: *Baseball's Biggest Bloopers, Baseball's Greatest Games, Baseball Babylon, World Series Classics* (all Viking), *They Came from Centerfield* (Scholastic), and *Banana Bats & Ding-Dong Balls* (Macmillan).

You may have seen Dan's articles in *Sports Illustrated for Kids, Highlights for Children, Esquire, Newsweek, USA Today, Discover, Science Digest, The Philadelphia Inquirer, The Village Voice*, and other publications. He also gives talks in schools.

Dan lives in Haddonfield, New Jersey with his wife Nina, his son Sam, and his daughter Emma. He is currently working on a book about gymnastics.

INDEX

Illustrations are indicated by boldface